george barber

george barber

with essays by gareth evans and paul morley

film and video umbrella

minigraph 8

First published 2005 by Film and Video Umbrella
52 Bermondsey Street London SE1 3UD
Tel: 020 7407 7755
Fax: 020 7407 7766
HTTP://www.fvumbrella.com

film and video umbrella 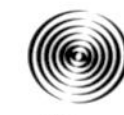 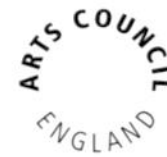 THE SURREY INSTITUTE OF ART & DESIGN UNIVERSITY COLLEGE

This publication was supported by a Grants for Arts award from
Arts Council England, London, and received additional support from
Surrey Institute of Art and Design

ISBN 1 90427 018 2

Edited by Steven Bode and Nina Ernst
Design by Claudia Schenk
Printed and bound by Graphicom, Italy

British Library Cataloguing in Publication Data: a CIP record for this
publication is available from the British Library

contents

the boy from georgetown 6

yes frank, no smoke 10

1001 colours andy never thought of 14

withdrawal 16

upside down minutiae 18

walking off court 20

shouting match 22

tilt 26

scratch free state 30

branson 32

absence of satan 34

ever happen, no? 38

passing ship 40

waiting for dave 44

i was once involved in a shit show 46

river sky 48

george barber: if you like, you can repeat the search with the omitted results included 52

lists 76

the boy from georgetown

gareth evans

The consensus on the work of video artist George Barber is that it falls comfortably into two distinct genres. The first of these centres on his pioneering and extremely influential 'scratch videos' (such as *Absence of Satan*, *Tilt* and *Yes Frank, No Smoke*) — bravura sound-and-image confections using appropriated and re-edited footage, whose visual élan and feel for music and syncopation is also found in a related series of more or less abstract or patterned pieces (*1001 Colours Andy Never Thought Of*, *Arizona*, *Effervescence* etc). A second, parallel strand of activity, on the other hand, revolves around a number of narrative micro-dramas, generally in monologue form — works such as *Walking Off Court*, *Passing Ship* or *The Venetian Ghost*, which take a moment in Barber's or another's life and, by describing it in some detail, reach out towards larger, shared truths about the nature and challenge of being human. These, and a concurrent series of real-world physical 'experiments' – resolutely actual, unmediated events in which individuals are pitched into everything from extreme shouting contests to inverse suspension from vehicles (*Shouting Match*, *Upside Down Minutiae*) – are also distinguished by the way they reveal the nature of their construction, but are each many miles away from the manipulated virtuality of his scratch tapes' pop-cultural source material.

Underneath this (all-too) neat schema, however, are shared, often overlapping, preoccupations and themes. Prominent among these is an emphasis on the contingent nature of 'truth' and perception, whether expressed in the deconstructive basis of the scratch video works or via the eccentric, unreliable narrators of *Refusing Potatoes* and *I Was Once Involved in a Shit Show*. There is also an ongoing tension between image and experience, between self-determination and the alienating effects of modern commercialised life, which is manifest in the normally concealed pressures of *Walking Off Court* or the parodic escapes of *Taxi Driver II*. This, and a certain eye for the fugitive beauty and latent possibilities of the discarded and overlooked (whether demonstrated in the use of junk material in the scratch works or in the throwaway asides of the monologue/narrative pieces) makes Barber's body of work fit together in a way that belies its surface differences.

In an essay published early in 2005 by the independent

British magazine *Filmwaves*, Barber traces a remarkably candid picture of his development as an artist while offering equally illuminating insights into some of the autobiographical roots of his work. This voluntary disclosure of personal details seems to invite us to consider his early years in the aptly named Georgetown, Guyana, as a kind of carefree childhood idyll, in which his infant wandering through the vibrant light and dazzling colours of the city that mirrors his name translates itself, in his later artistic life, into an equally relaxed appropriation of images from the wider territories of media and cinema.

Similarly, when his Caribbean idyll was abruptly curtailed with relocation to grim private schooling in England, you can sense him chafing against these newly imposed social codes and hierarchical systems of control and, like many others before him, transforming them into a tellingly creative subversion (think again of *Taxi Driver II* and the poignancy of its 'Englishness', its Perrinesque modesty). In his calm, amused delivery, Barber comes across as a particularly convivial tour guide of cultural detritus (with its attendant, surreptitious beauties) as well as an understated map-bearer of possible ways out of the socio-spiritual slum. Gleaning eagerly on the landfill sites of contemporary culture and with an equally sharp ear and eye for archaic, obsolete phrasings or marginal individual storylines, he's in search of the shard (material, mental or metaphorical) that catches the sun on a brisk and bright day's outing. It might be the filmic or experiential equivalent of a tin can rusted almost completely to the colour of an old boot, but under the right gaze it becomes the snatch of gold dropped by a hightailing partisan after a rush run on the provincial vault. Either way, litter or loot, there is a moment of surprised glory in it.

Scratch, this re-ordering of popular artefacts, of *thin* images, into something stranger and more ambiguous, was, and in many ways still *is*, the perfect tool for the times. It both satirises and salvages, pleases and provokes. It offers a carnival parade of icons and images, where the holding of power briefly changes, becomes democratised and diverse. Rhythmic, electric-hued, passing from the street to onward gaze, the carnival becomes resistance, first by simply being, and only then, once it has been experienced, by how it can be read.

Barber's use of a sampling technology that encourages the subversion both of itself and the values (consumer and otherwise) that have bought it into being, can be seen to echo some similarly seismic shifts in contemporary art, where production and ownership are unstable elements of a process that does not necessarily result in a saleable artefact. Barber is more interested in tagging, graffiti-style, the images that he finds, signing them off with his own intervention, rather than claiming any fresh ownership. Often taken from star actor vehicles, these image sequences become, under Barber, a brake on the mass-produced image environment, not least because they challenge, in video, the idea that an artist must bring a wholly new artefact into the world.

Scratch codes its own will to reuse and recycle into the very veins of its aesthetic. It looks deeper and closer at what is already here and made, seeking revelations of wide import in the most trivial exchanges of bad acting, dialogue or staging. It is intended to view the world differently, to avoid automatism. It is a call to re-imagine the common arenas of perception and experience, in both virtual and real-world spaces; to shuffle the co-ordinates, as Julio Cortázar's *Hopscotch* (1966) and BS Johnson's *The Unfortunates* (1969) did for the written page of the novel.

From Barber's early cut-ups, to the dynamic camera and protagonist movements of the performance films and the inverted gaze of the harness volunteers, things are given a shake and stir, all the better to perceive reality as it could be, or is already, elsewhere. Upside down, our conventional priorities are usurped. If only we knew how to look. And this new looking seeks to reclaim lost control — individually, collectively, artistically and ethically; to fight the powerlessness of living near motorways, being tugged and shoved in shouting seats, neutered by answerphones, tied up and swung. It's about taking the means of production to change what the production means. In this sense, scratch and its later performative compadres make a utopian proposal.

• • •

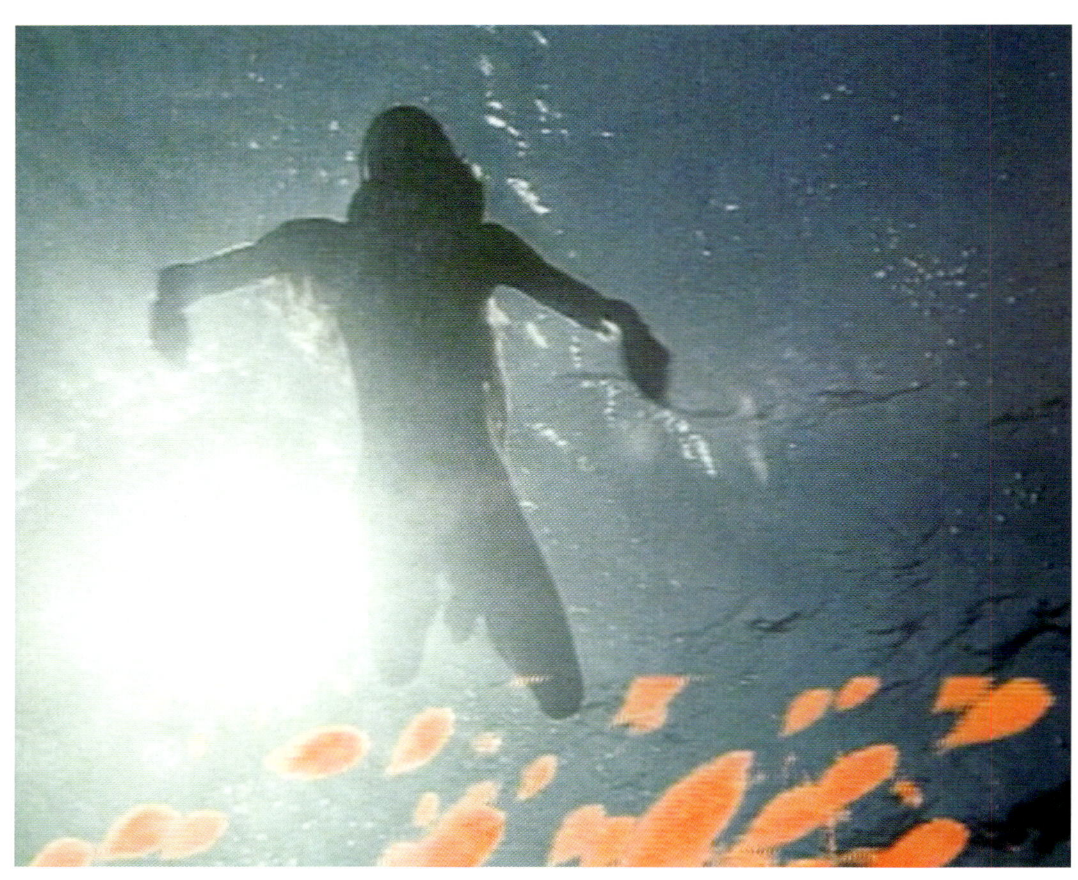

It's no accident that the primary, and driving, samples in *Yes Frank, No Smoke*, Barber's densely woven masterwork of scratch, come from that staple of television filler, *The Deep*. Feature film fodder that is anything but profound, this adaptation of the Peter Benchley novel nevertheless allows Barber both to make enjoyable verbal wordplay around the flotsam and jetsam of purely surface images while highlighting video's essential materiality. As Nick Nolte and Jacqueline Bisset swim naked through the tropical waters or knock (more than twice, of course…) on Robert Shaw's door, their actions remind us that video is, in a way, both wave and particle: a moment on tape that can be isolated and copied into high-rhythm repeats; and an almost marine environment, where actions, expressions, dialogue and sound exist in a swell of currents. It is entirely appropriate, then, that the whole work unfolds within another kind of ocean, a coloured ebb and flow of pixel wash. The cast of *The Deep* are joined by the young orphans of *The Blue Lagoon*, amongst others, all of whom share problems with communication, whether bad phone access or a constantly alternating 'yes' and 'no'. Roy Scheider's gifting of Barber's title becomes an articulate – but narratively concise – summary of scratch's impulse to call and response, whether verbal or visual.

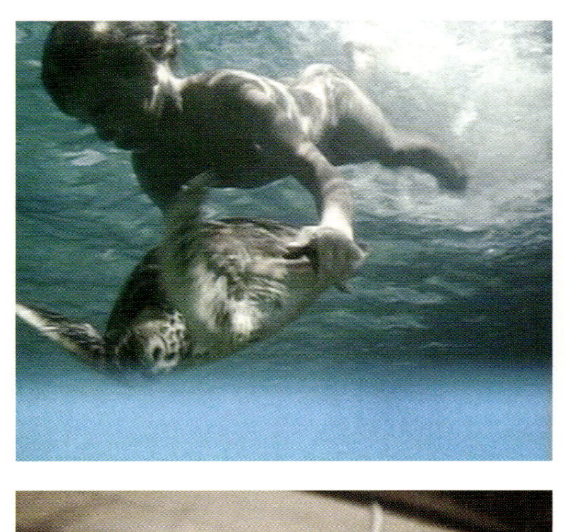
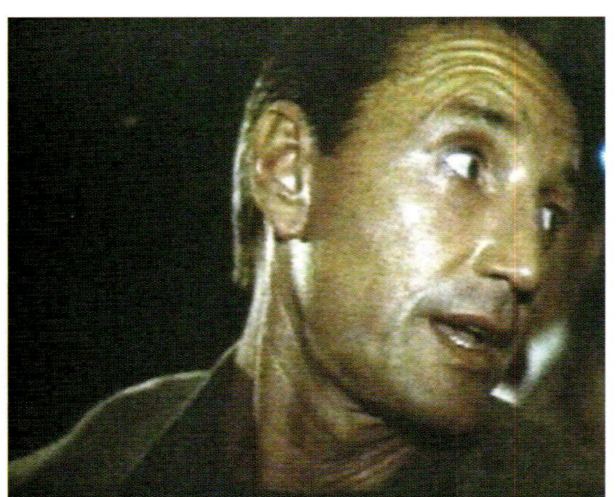
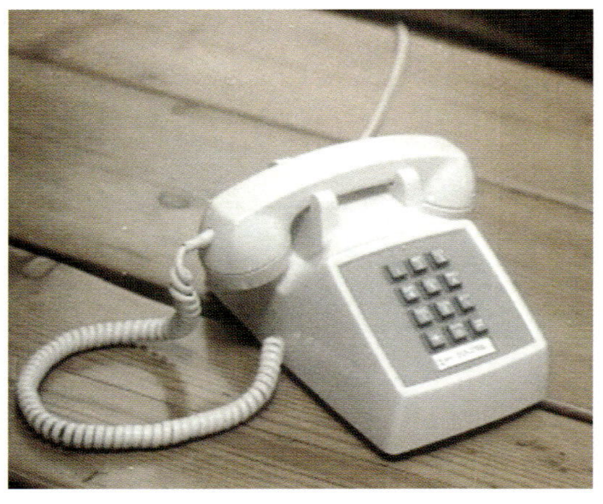
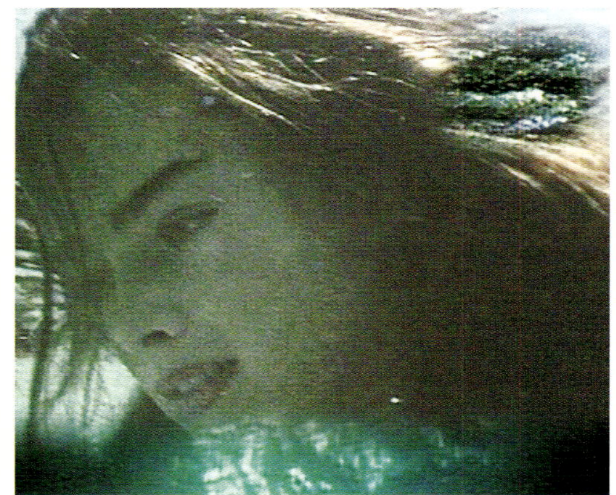

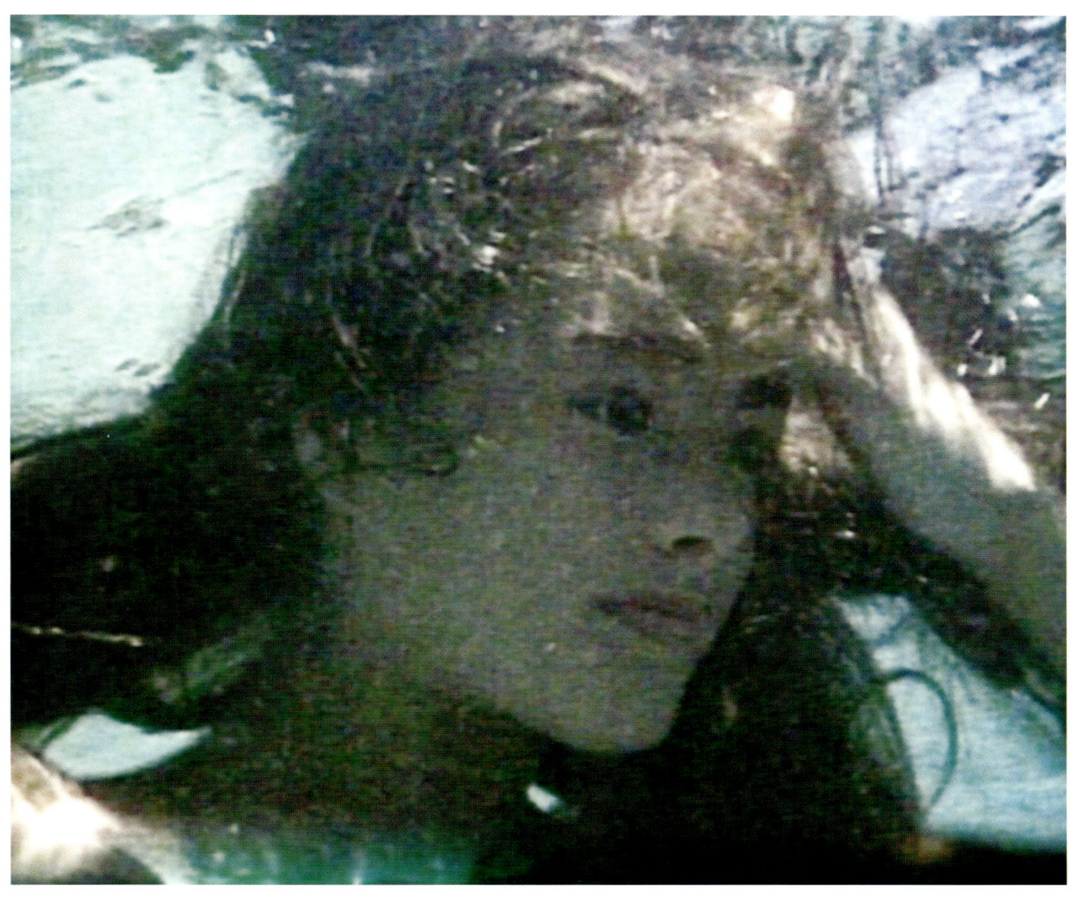

That Andy Warhol's appropriation and redirection of the mass-market artefact would appeal to Barber is of little surprise. In *1001 Colours Andy Never Thought Of*, his take on Warhol's *Marilyn* (1962) – a homage to the artist who in a sense originated the scratch technique, albeit in a different medium – brings the fluidity of video dissolves to the fixed material dimensions of the original image. Using wipes of saturated colour across the face of the iconic actress – a constantly changing visage of multiple garish hues scored to dreamy electronica – Barber provides one of the clearest examples of his desire to be immersed in the abstracting potential of technology, a dream of the shifting surface that suggests the ephemerality of both subject and signal. Only his *Arizona*, with its landscape of morphing forms and ambient passages, delivers this particular strain of the Barber project as effectively.

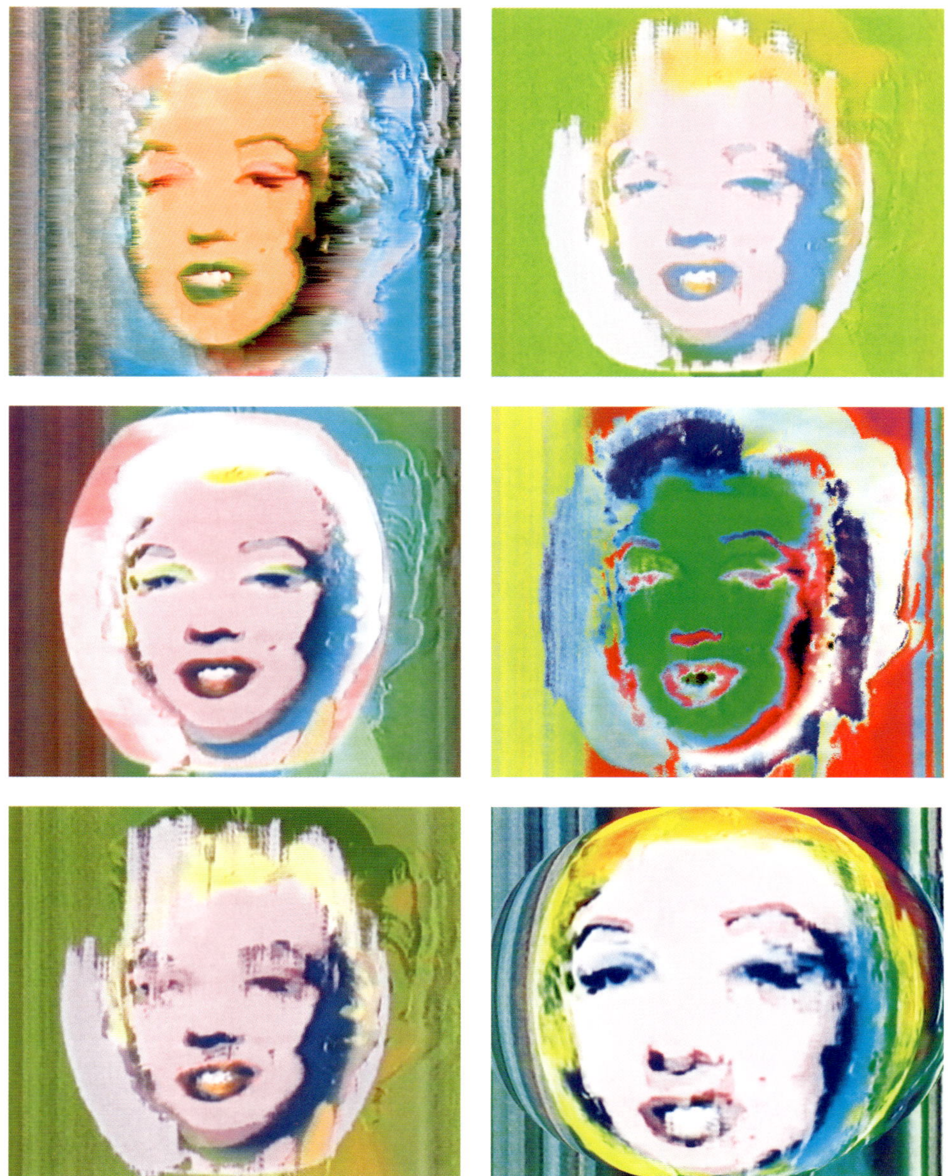

Another of Barber's works, *Withdrawal*, skilfully weaves the material with the metaphysical. Originally made for the Channel 4-supported experimental animation strand 'Animate!', a commission whose only prerequisite is some form of manipulation of the image, Barber's accumulating digital erasures, formally simple but thematically 'animating', fit the brief like a body does a coffin. Here we are presented with a seeming pastoral idyll, a green meadow stretching to trees and mountains beyond, all under the perfect blue of sky, its drifting clouds offering no threat of rain. In a series of short scenes, a relaxed (and probably extended) family group walk happily towards and past the camera. Each time they do so however, their number reduces, along with certain features of the landscape, until finally we are left with a single boy, walking on the earth itself, devoid of flora and foliage. Accompanying the entire progress have been fragments of dialogue on mortality and the passing of things from voices of all ages. As the boy leaves the frame for the last time, the camera pans slowly up from the empty planet to the constellations far above. The measuring of human time and its stories against such vastness is conveyed precisely and poignantly, with the sense, of course, that the universe itself is given meaning by those very creatures whose lives seem emblematic of insignificance. The narratives of stars do not diminish our being; rather they cast greater, lasting light on its value.

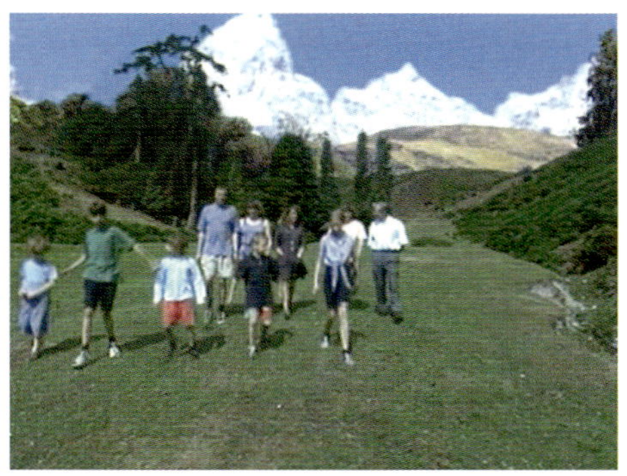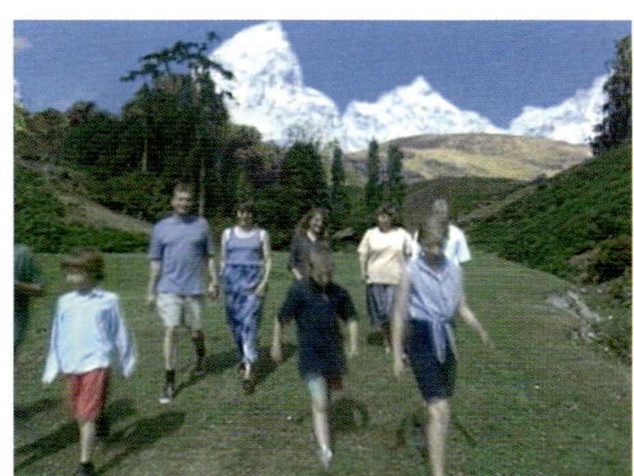

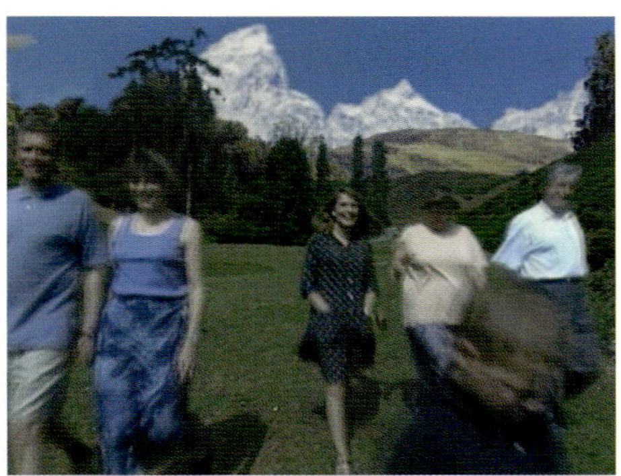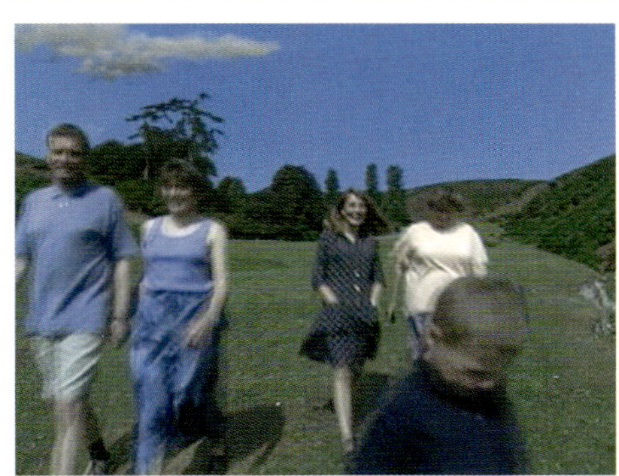

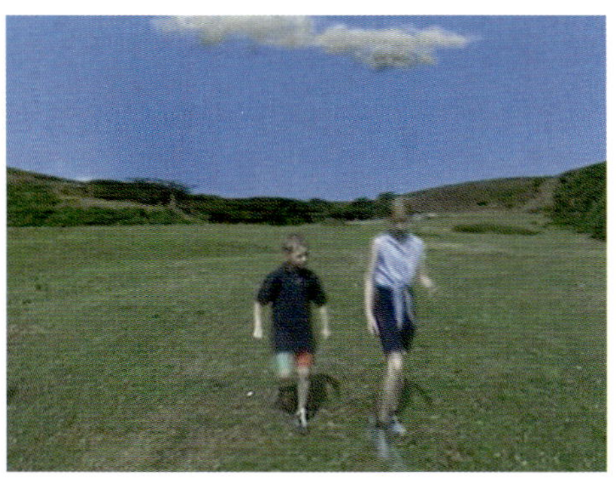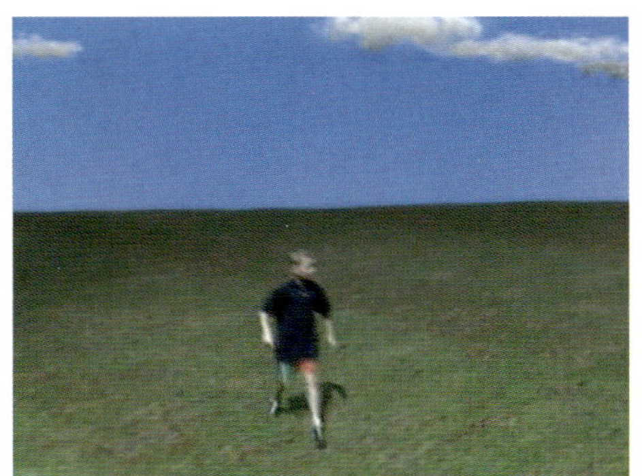

How we might be situated, as individuals, is considered also in *Upside Down Minutiae*. In this work, three individuals, strung upside down on a scaffolding frame attached to the back of a truck, are taken on a short drive around everyday streets, a microphone recording what they see and hear. Later the participants are interviewed by Barber, who asks them a series of personal questions about their childhood and other significant events in their lives that, with hindsight, they see in a different light. Is it too simple to suggest that this momentary repositioning of their bodies, in relation to the world as it is, has unlocked a previously inaccessible chamber of deep-seated responses? Could these rushes of blood to the head echo, albeit more optimistically, certain of the other jolts to reappraisal that surface throughout Barber's work? How does the beauty of the street foliage fit into all this? What is abundantly clear is that, yet again, Barber has managed to let us consider afresh the images and sites of our being, green shoots of thought bursting through the defaults we allow to dominate our actions and reactions.

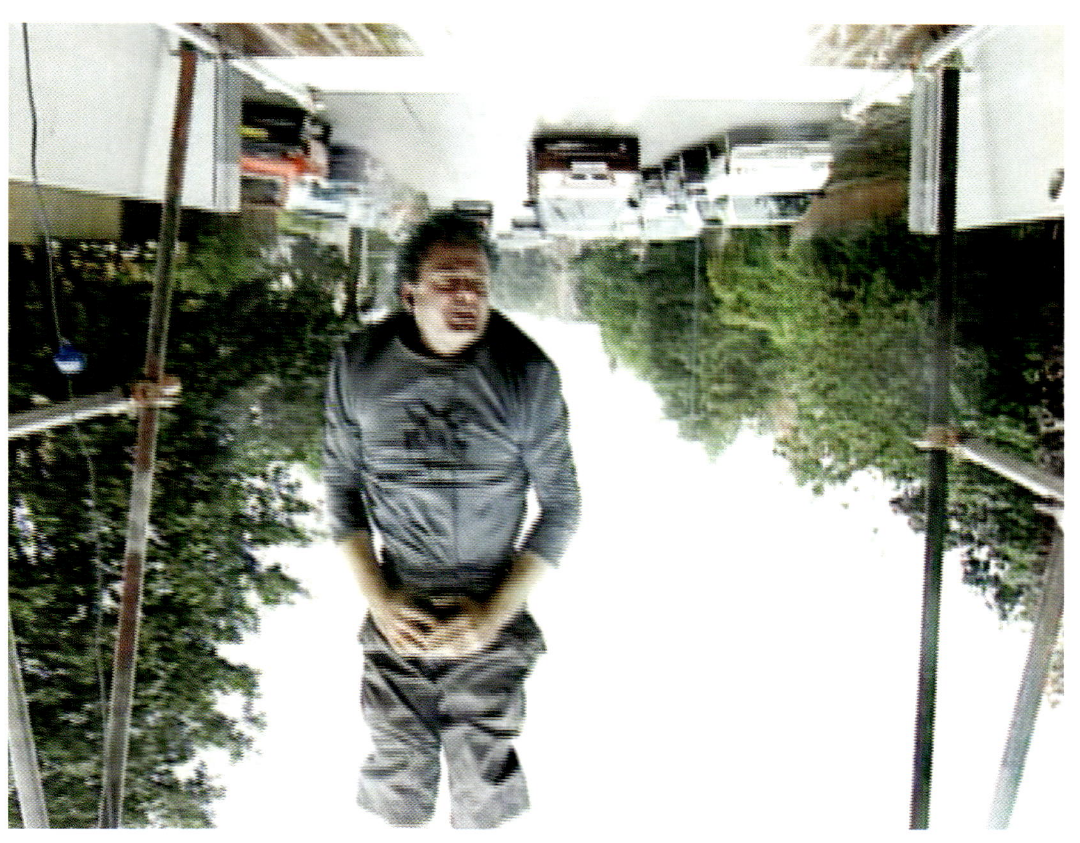

An epic of everyday loneliness and institutional oppression, Barber's understated 'road rage' drama, *Walking Off Court*, deploys 'big' music and sweeping, often inverted, panning shots to emphasise the significant emotions and psychological trauma concealed behind the concrete aprons of the suburban. Drawn from an article in *The Times* about a tennis pro's breakdown after a major motorway was built outside his house, the film is a quietly devastating attack on the various alienations created by modern life, whether the distancing nature of domestic technology (answerphones controlling, and blocking, all communication) or the monstrous insensitivity of bureaucracy and overwhelming infrastructure projects. As Barber narrates James Goodman's story, the fable of a man driven to crisis point by the road's construction and his inability to make contact with possible tennis partners, the camera arcs and dives like an extravagant top-spin lob or a high-kicking power serve, finally flipping completely as Goodman's universe is turned upside down. In a significant final shot, we find ourselves at the edge of the known world, down by the waterline on a gently sloping beach, as Barber ups the stakes to highlight parallels between tennis and the in/ability properly to live, even to survive as a species. What could be cod philosophising is poignantly anchored by the actual individual journey that has led us to this point, and closes one of Barber's most significant enquiries into the melancholy nature of things.

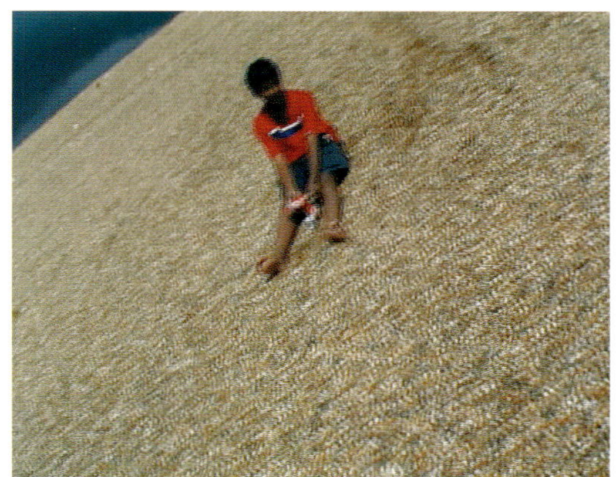

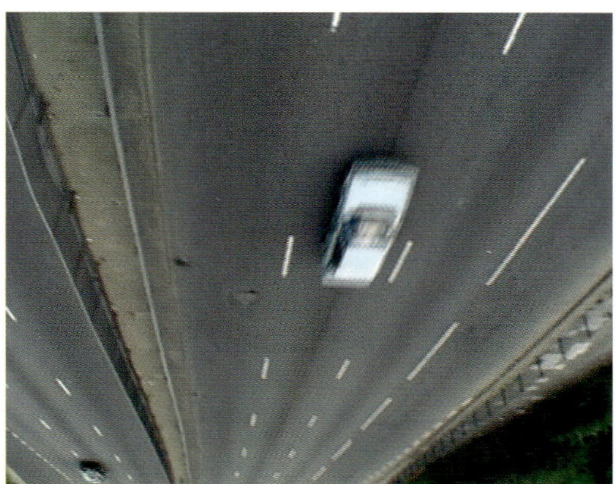

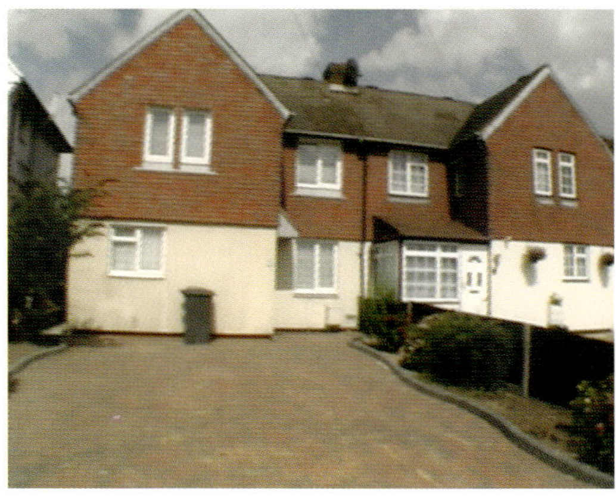

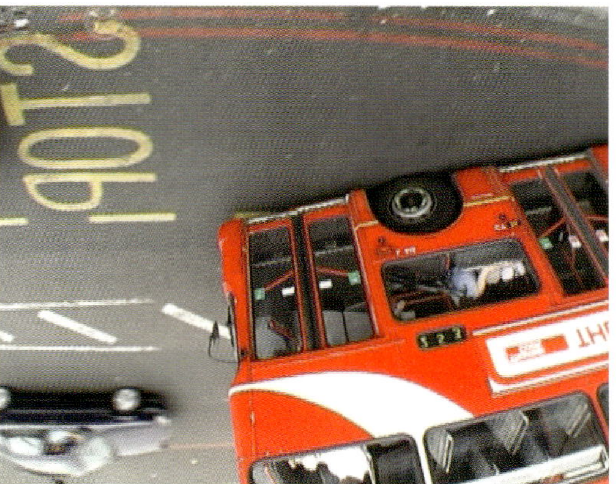

A comparable sense of alienation can be found in *Shouting Match*, the most recent of Barber's endurance films and the leftfield cousin of the environmental artifices prevalent in so much 'Reality TV' programming. Here contestants converge on the abandoned shell of a former supermarket, caught in the limbo of ring roads and retail parks, in order to shout at each other in a highly orchestrated competitive ritual that could perhaps be considered a 'Rollerball' of the throat. Strapped into chairs that run on rails towards each other, and propelled forward or back by off-screen volunteers, the contestants seek to out-shout their opponent, thus remaining in-frame, in the action. As the clock ticks from day to dusk and beyond, in a low-rent nod to the durational aspect of 'reality' machinations, the scenario becomes both a perfect metaphor for the underlying nature of much archetypal human behaviour and a deceptively simple incarnation of the forward impulse of contemporary cultural, social and political exchange. More Nau-man than New Man, *Shouting Match* also throws down the gauntlet to broadcast television. Barber's quiet, private dream is perhaps that certain of his filmic 'exercises' become the springboard for an entirely new wave of celebrity involvement in the mediated spectacle, the pillories of the post-modern. And why not? Surely it's just the case that Barber, in his relaxed generosity, would be 'giving something back'.

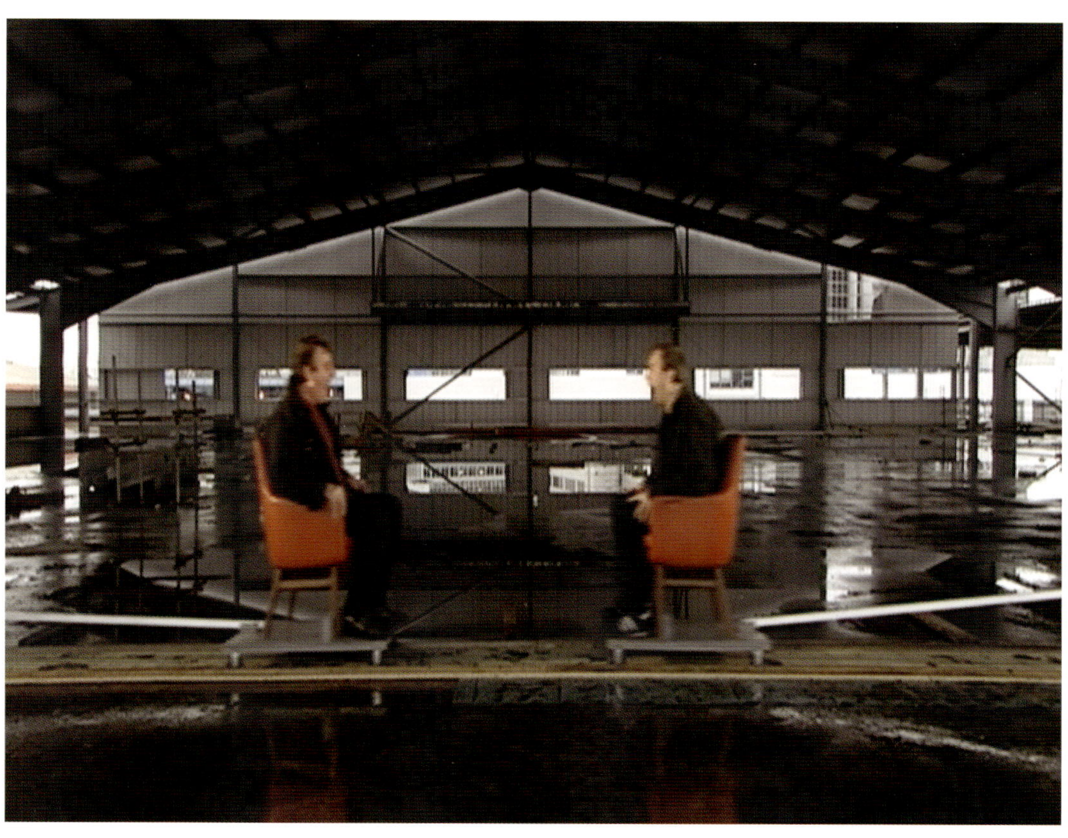

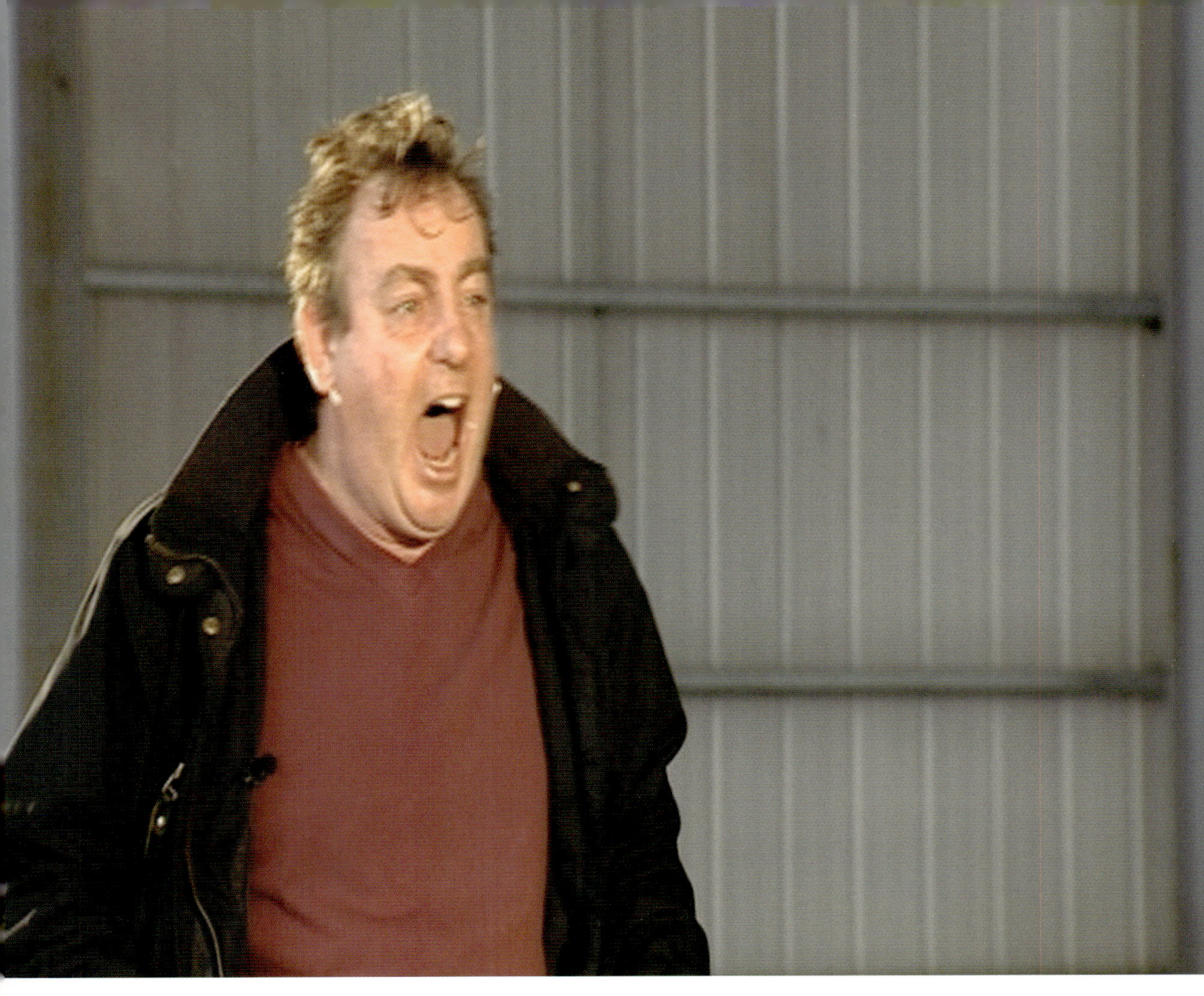

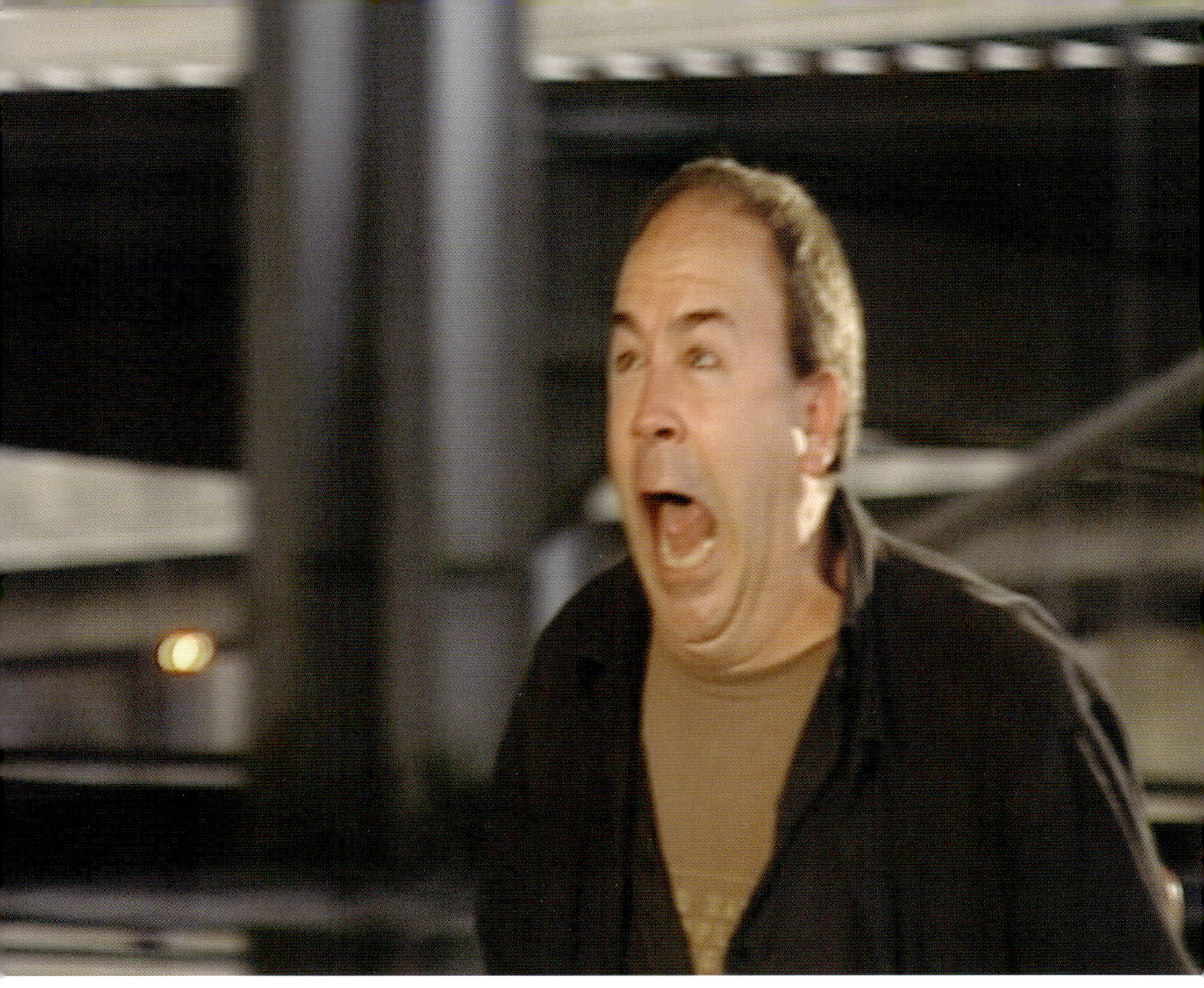

tilt

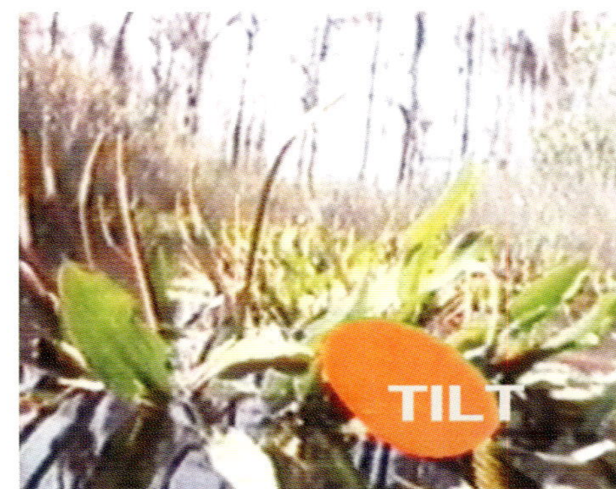

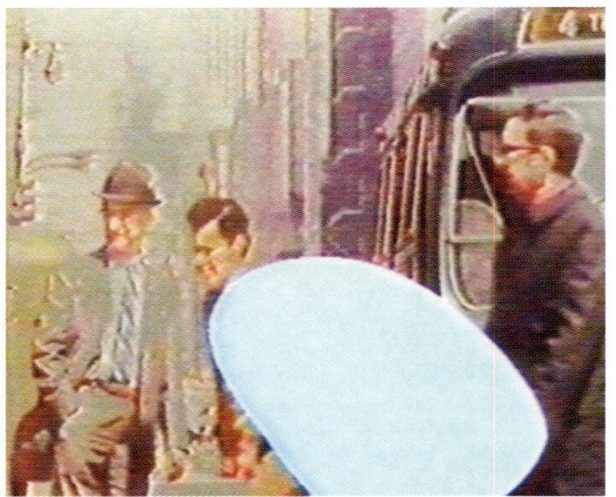

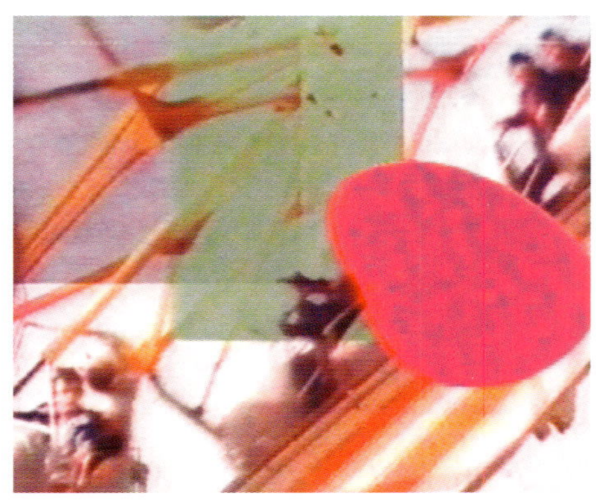

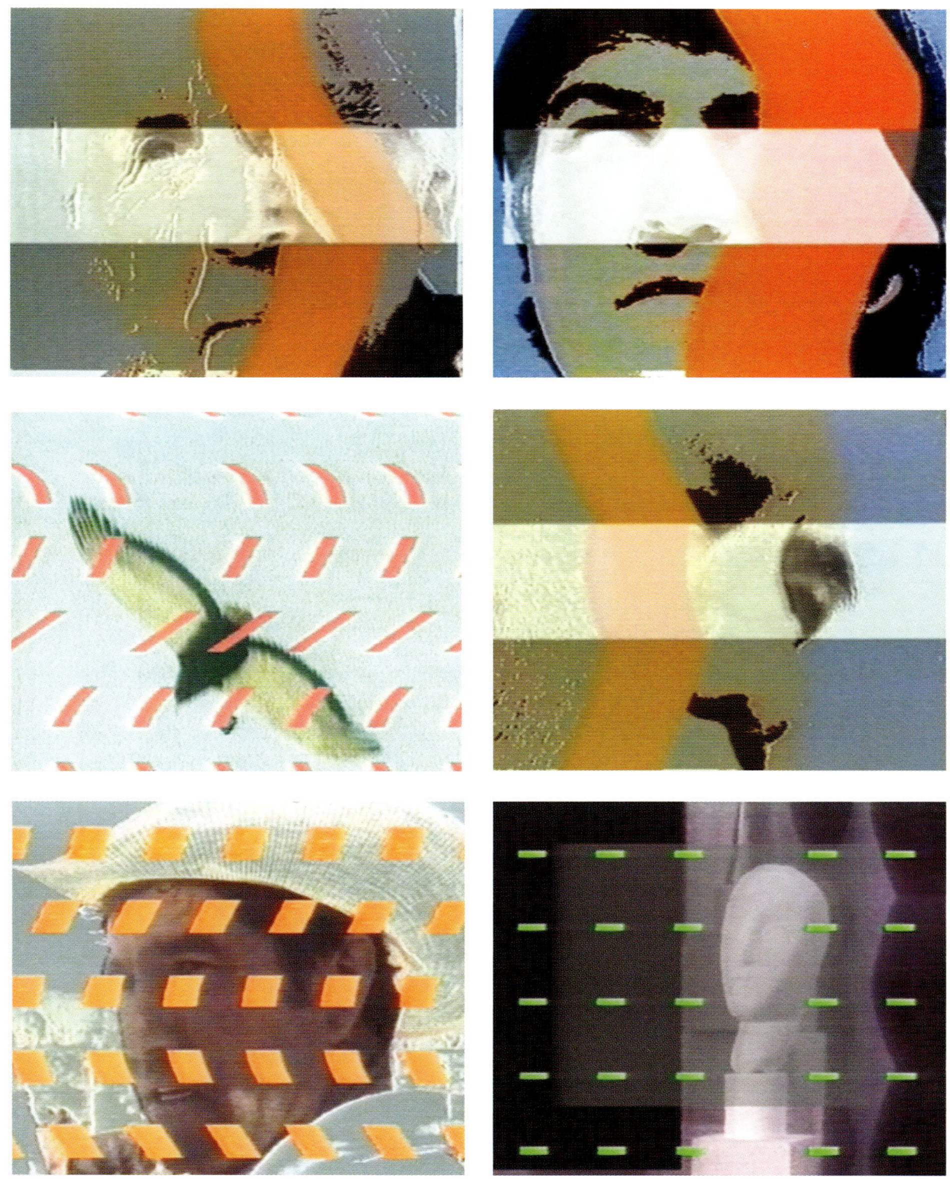

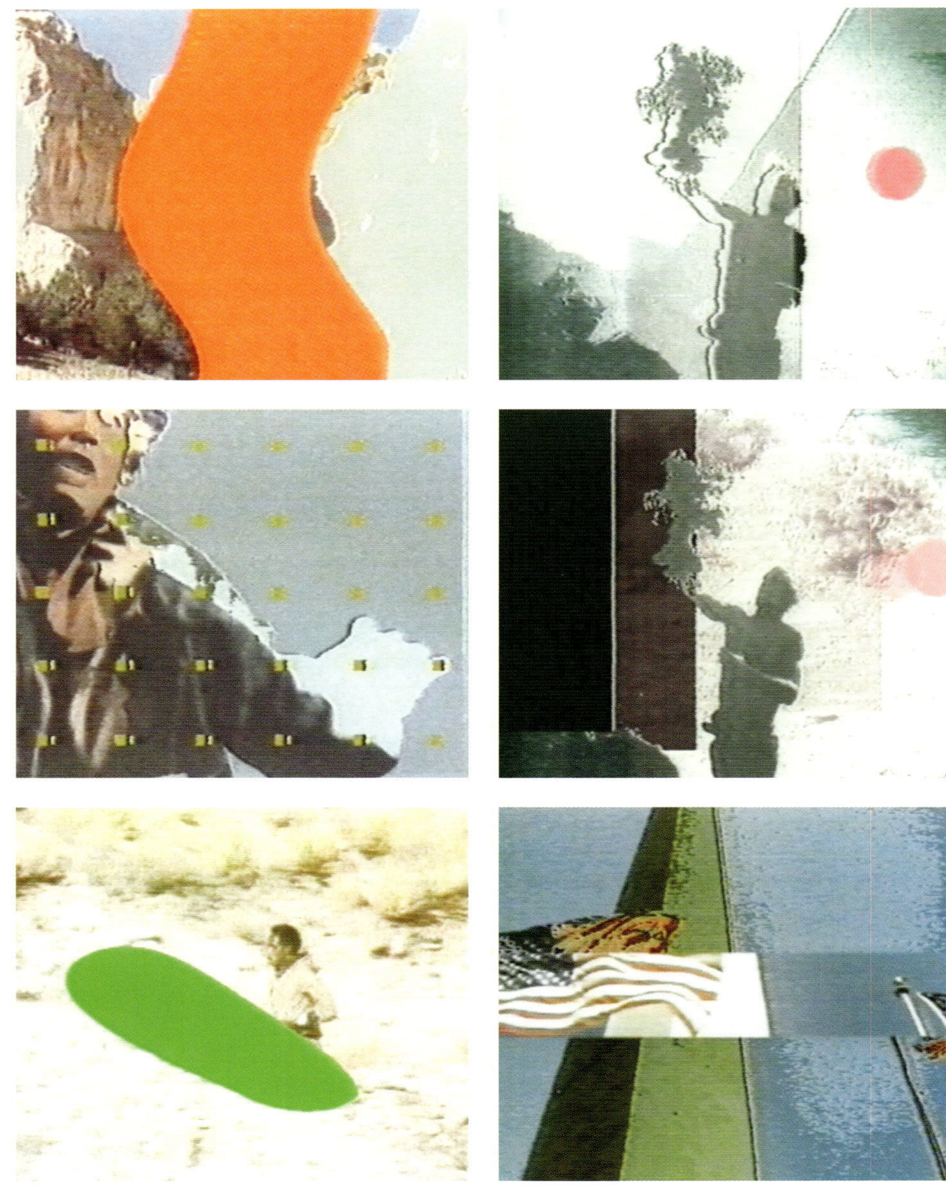

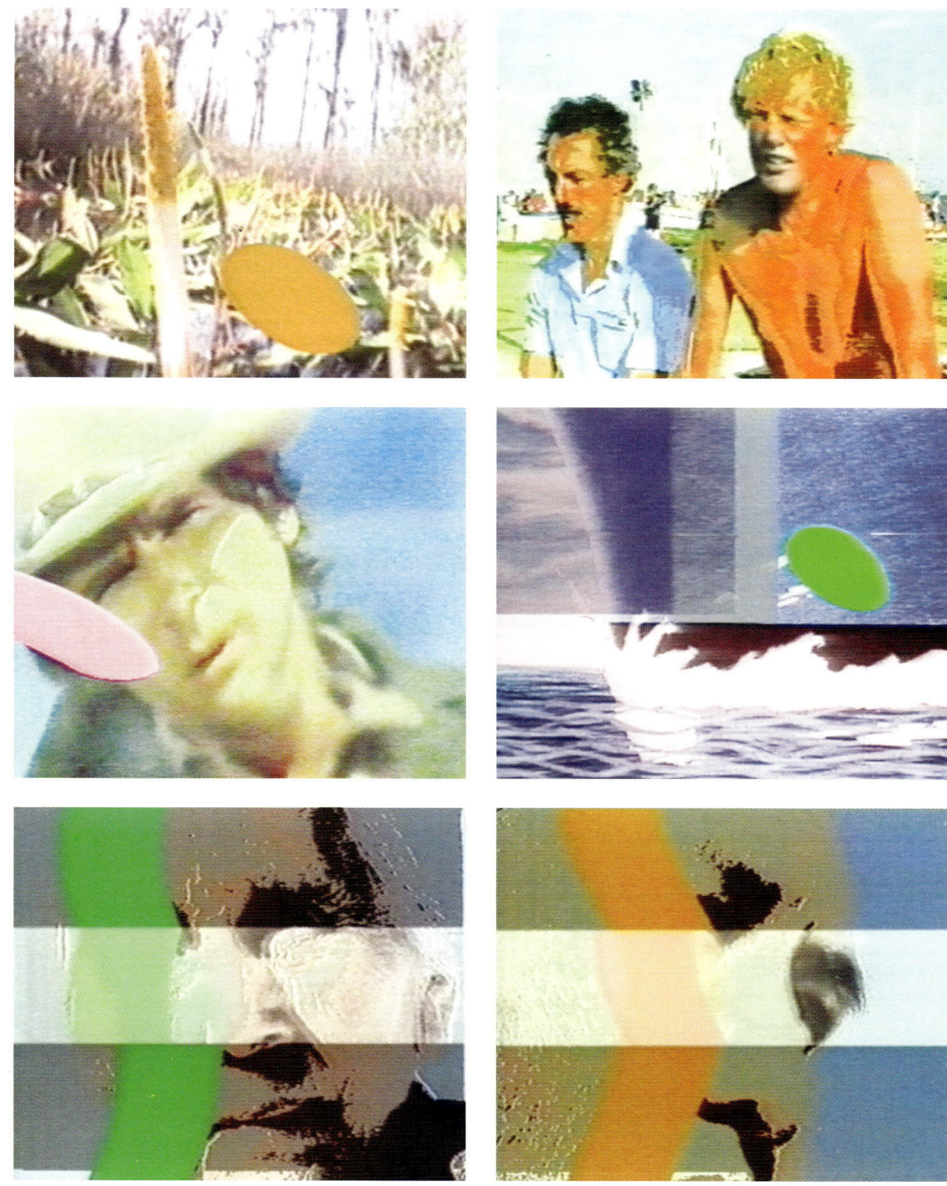

scratch free state

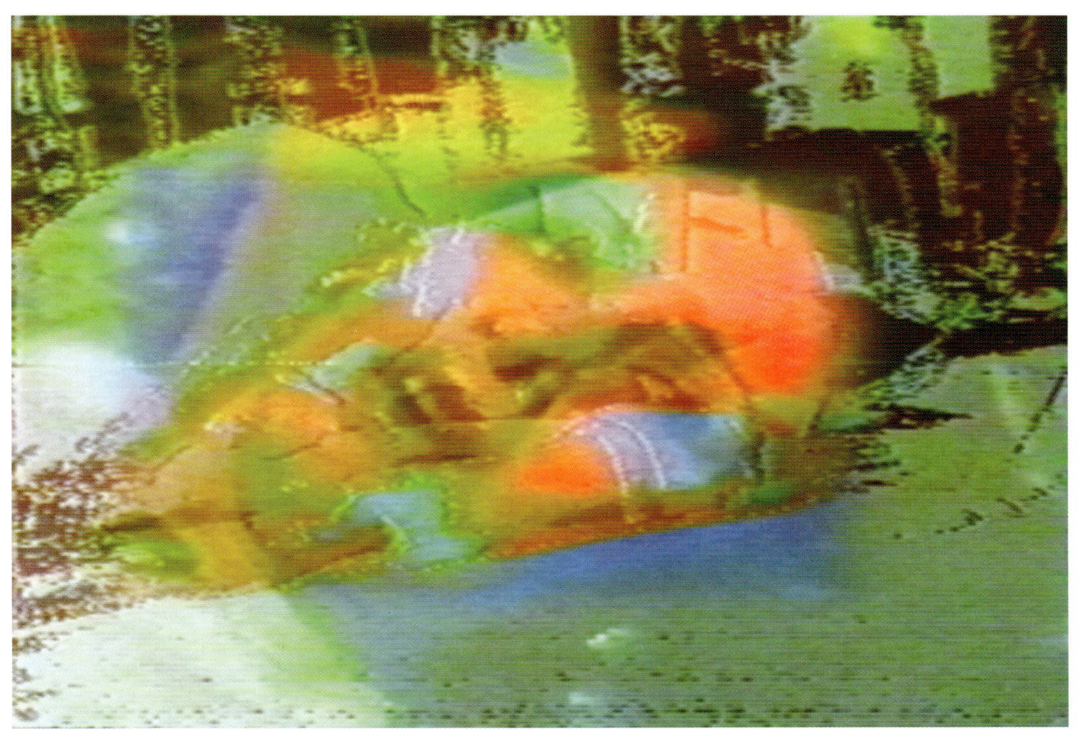

branson

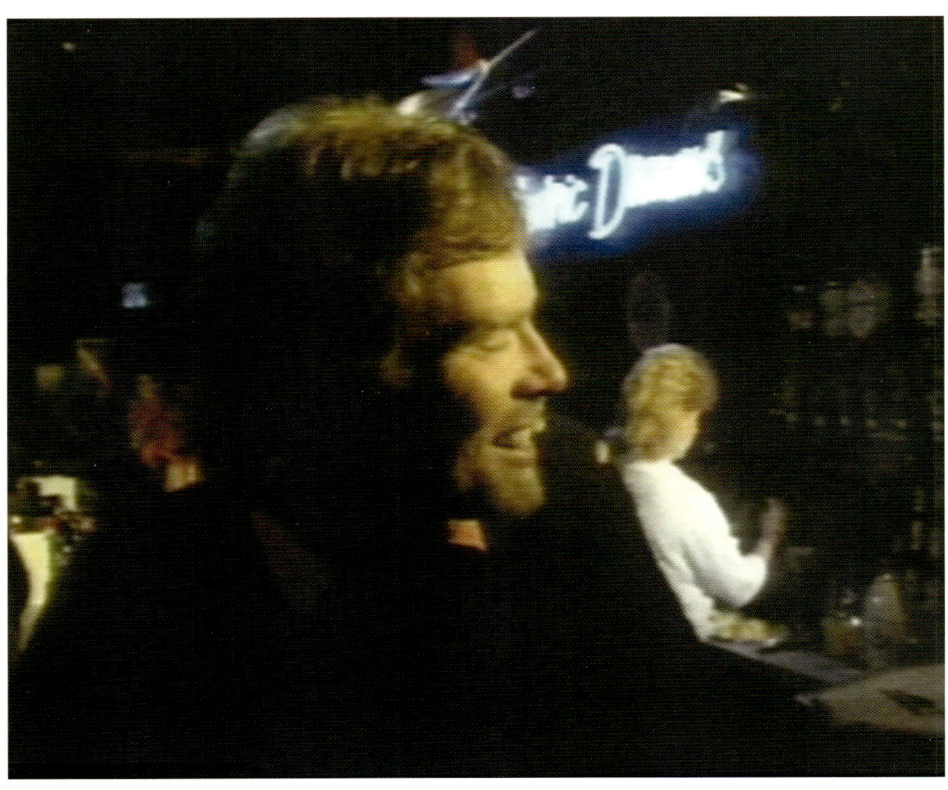

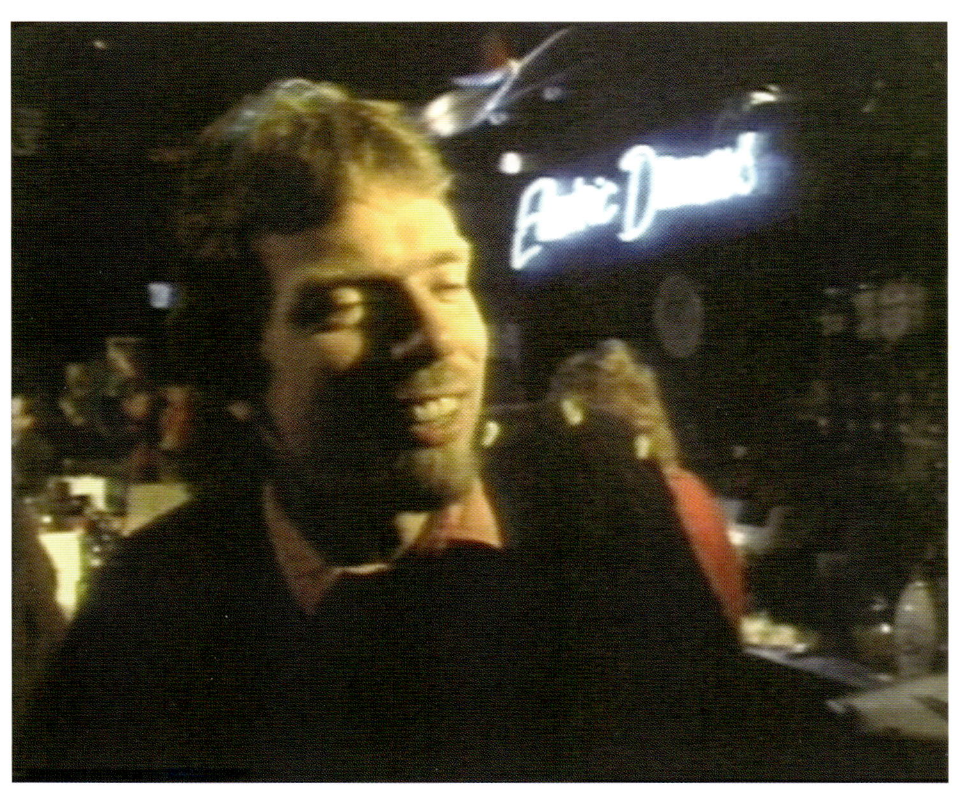

absence of satan

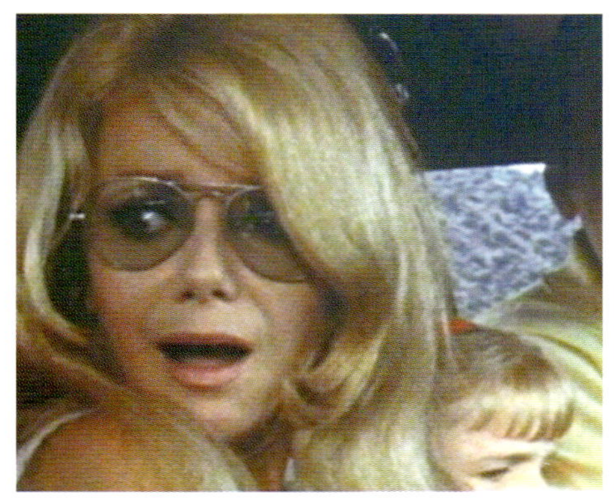 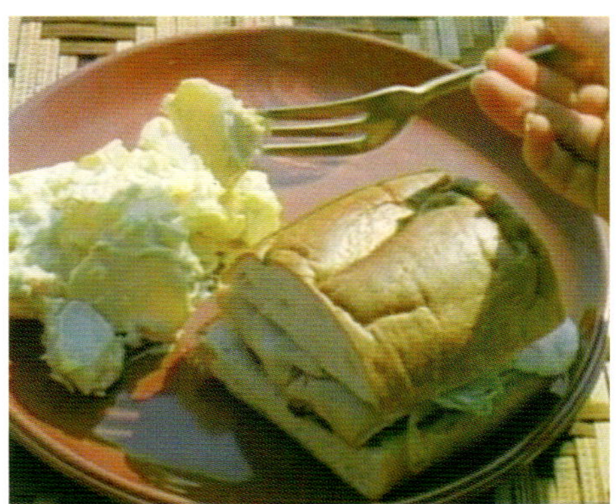

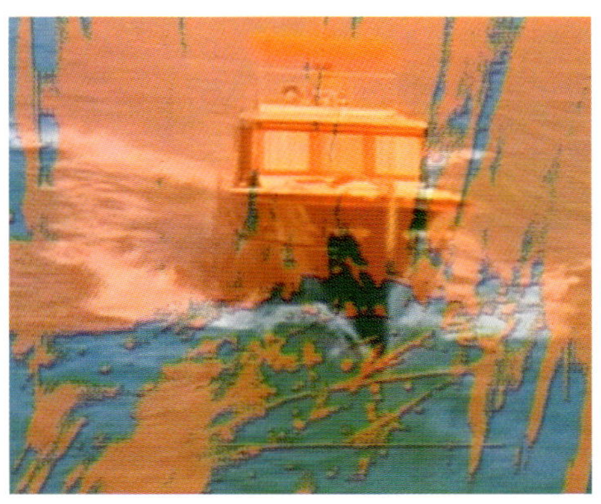 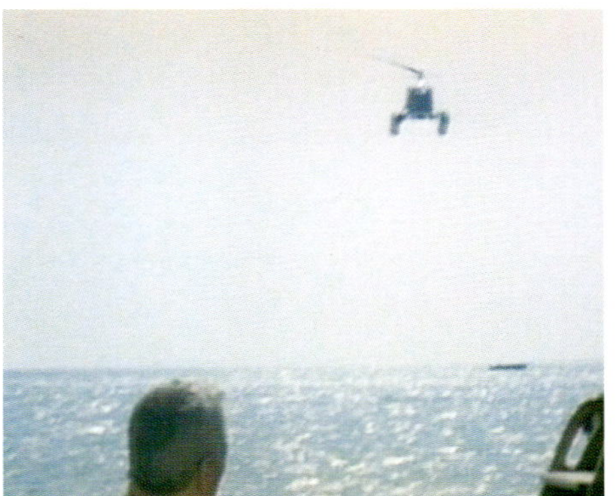

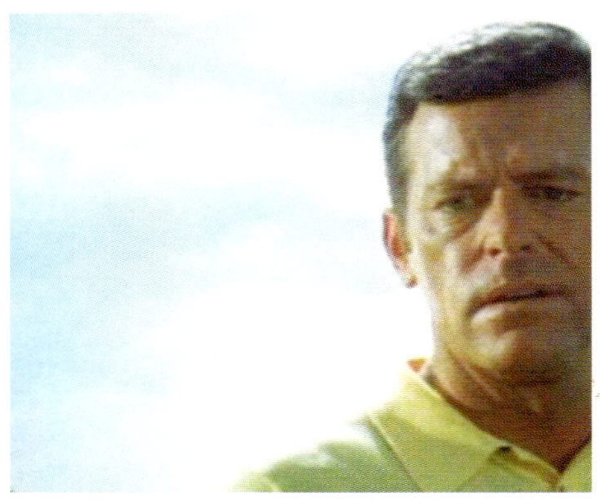 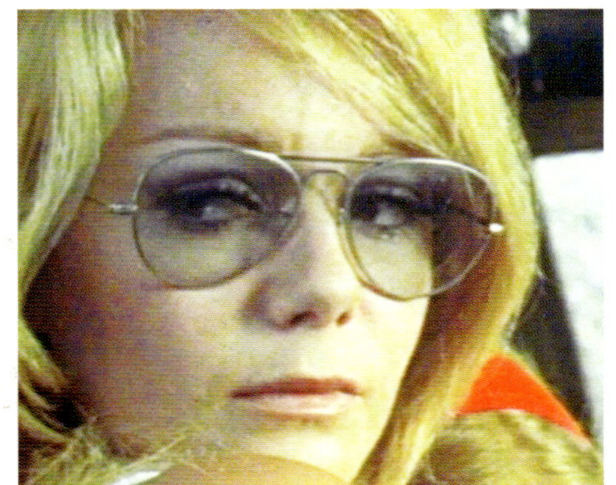

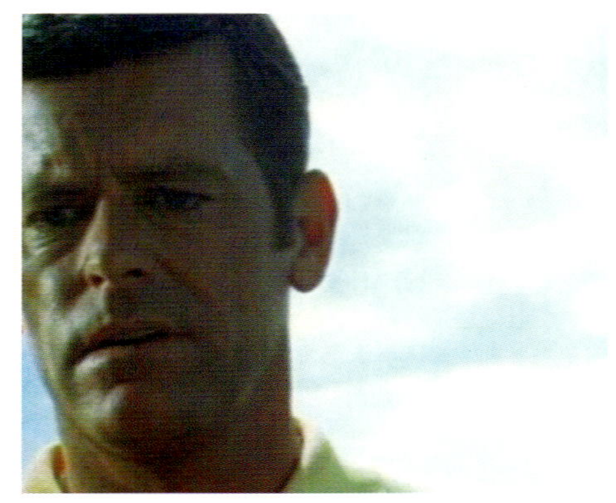
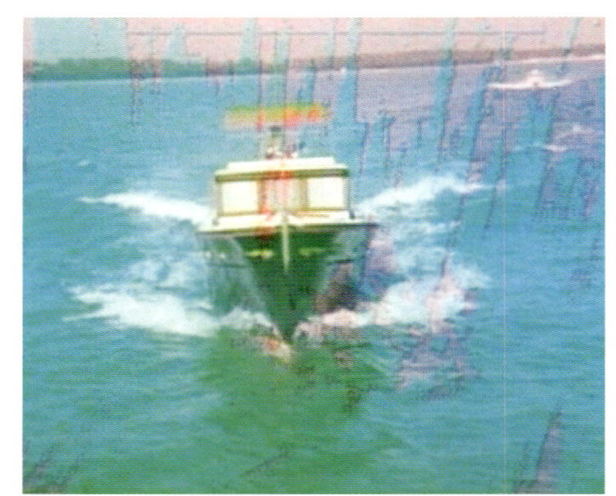
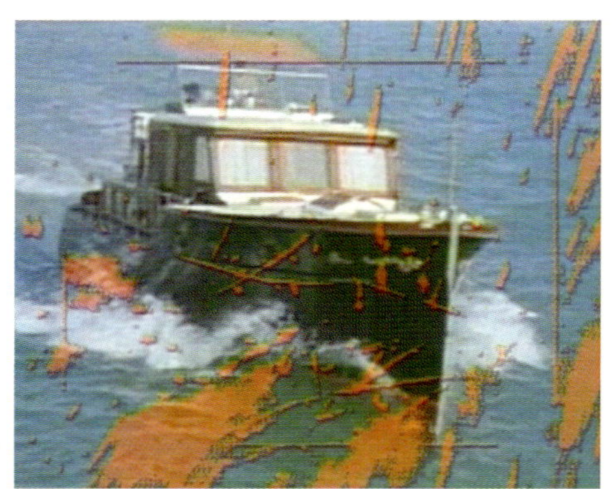
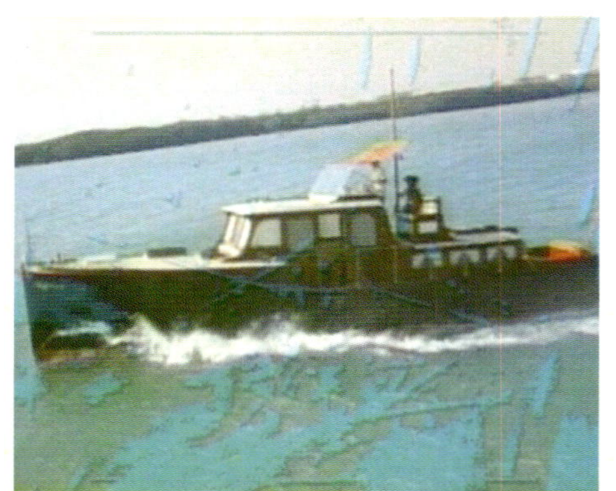
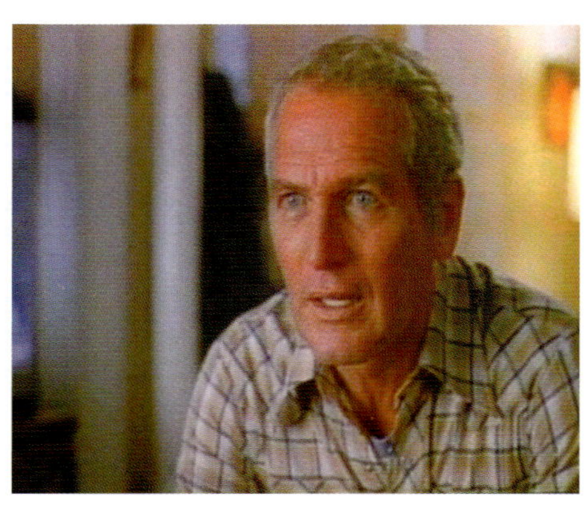
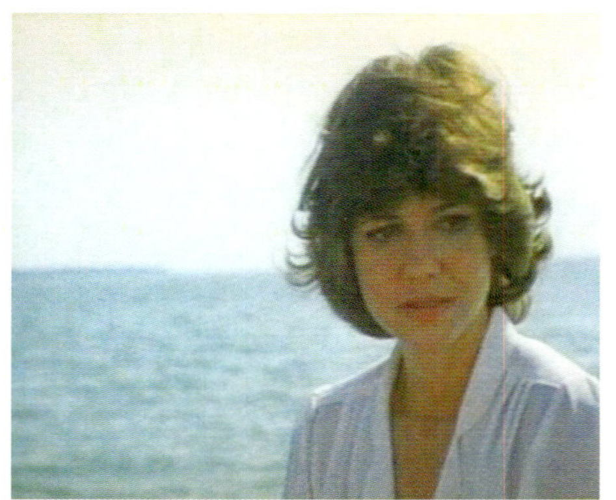

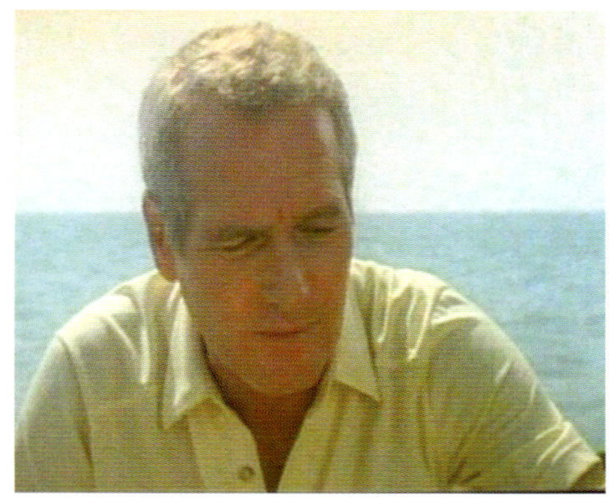
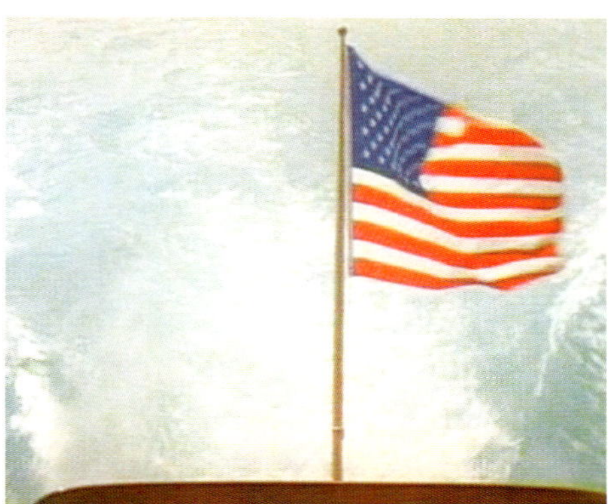
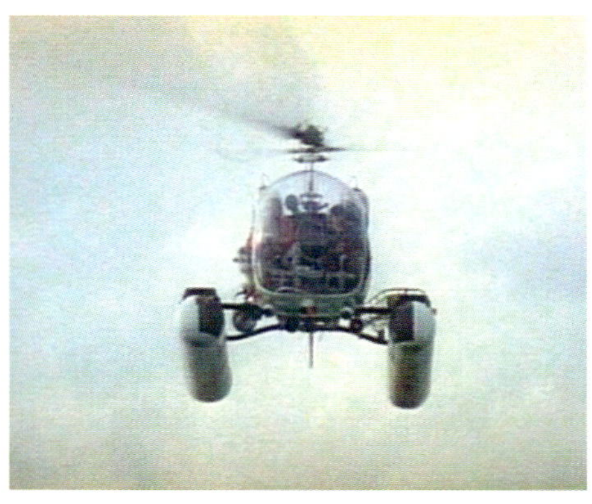
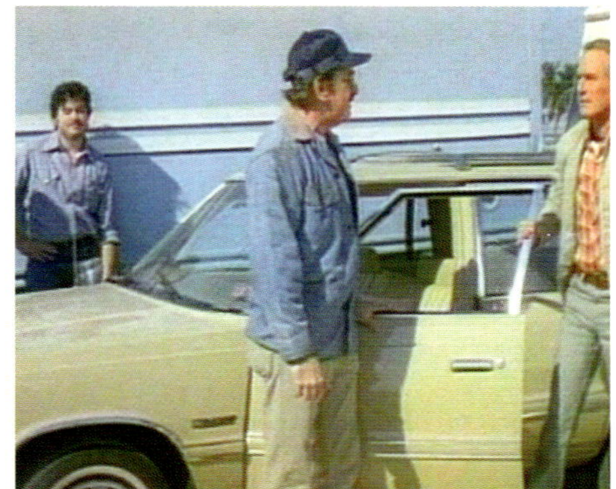
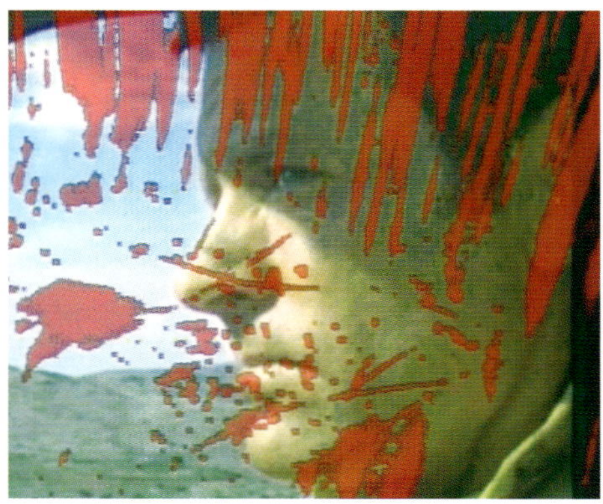
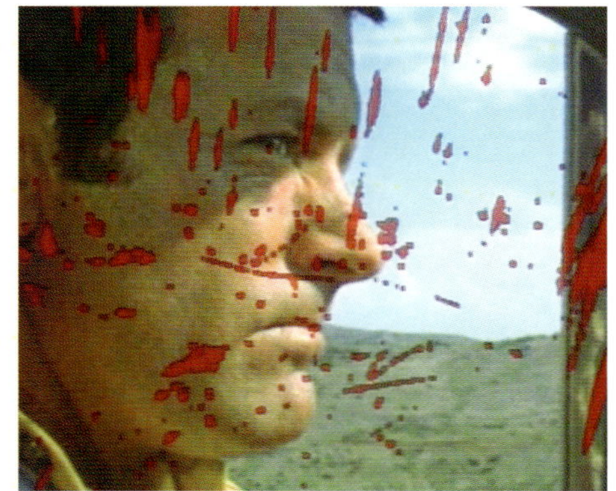

ever happen, no?

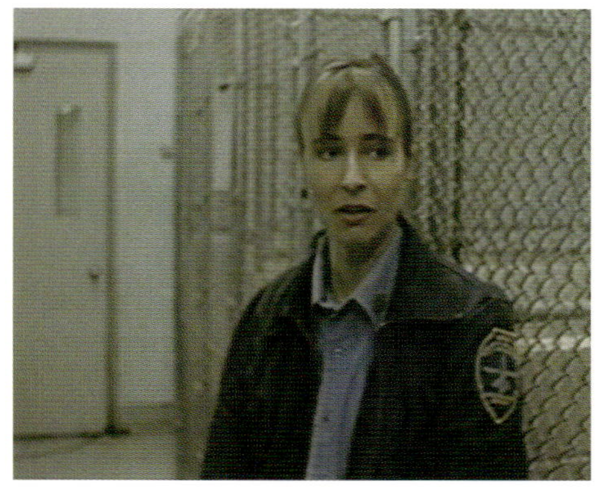

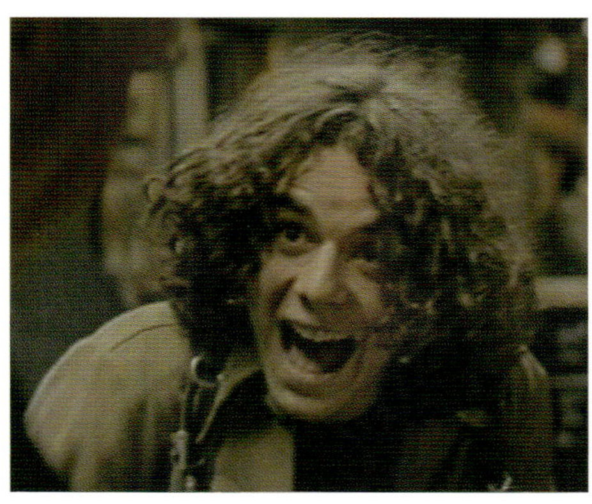
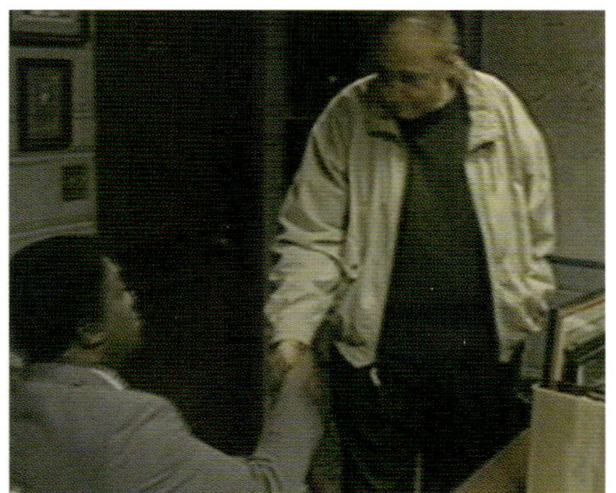

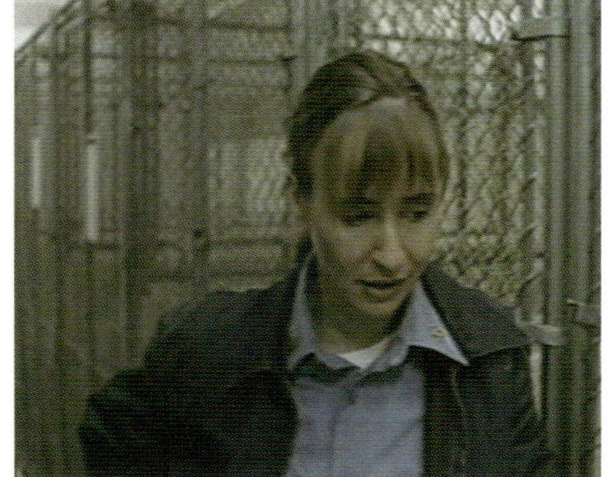

passing ship

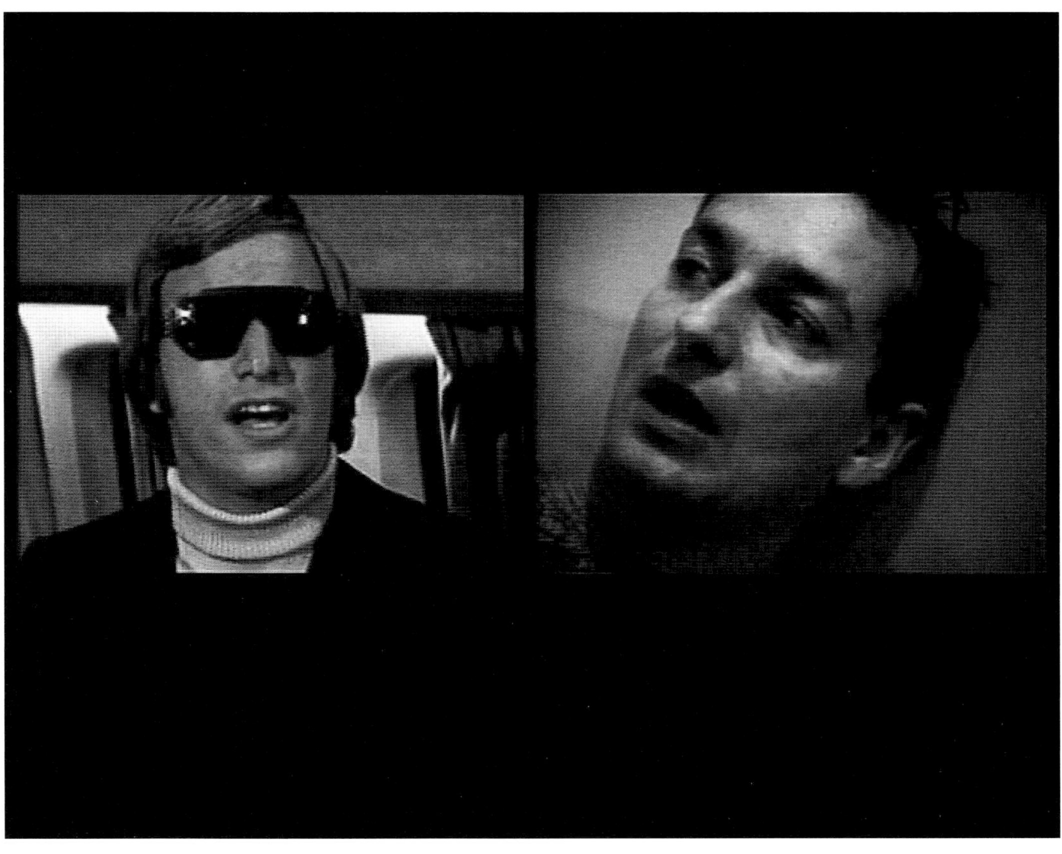

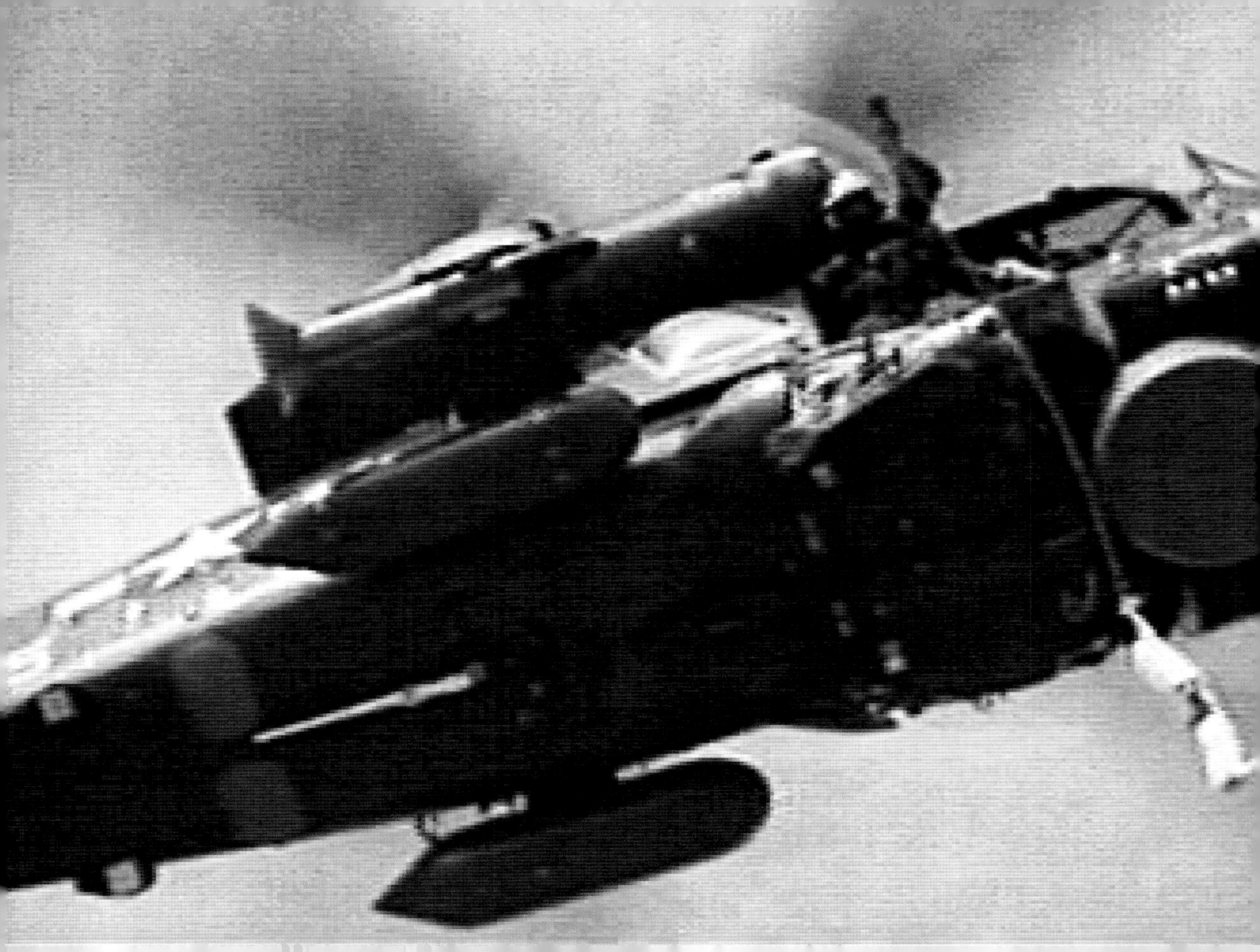

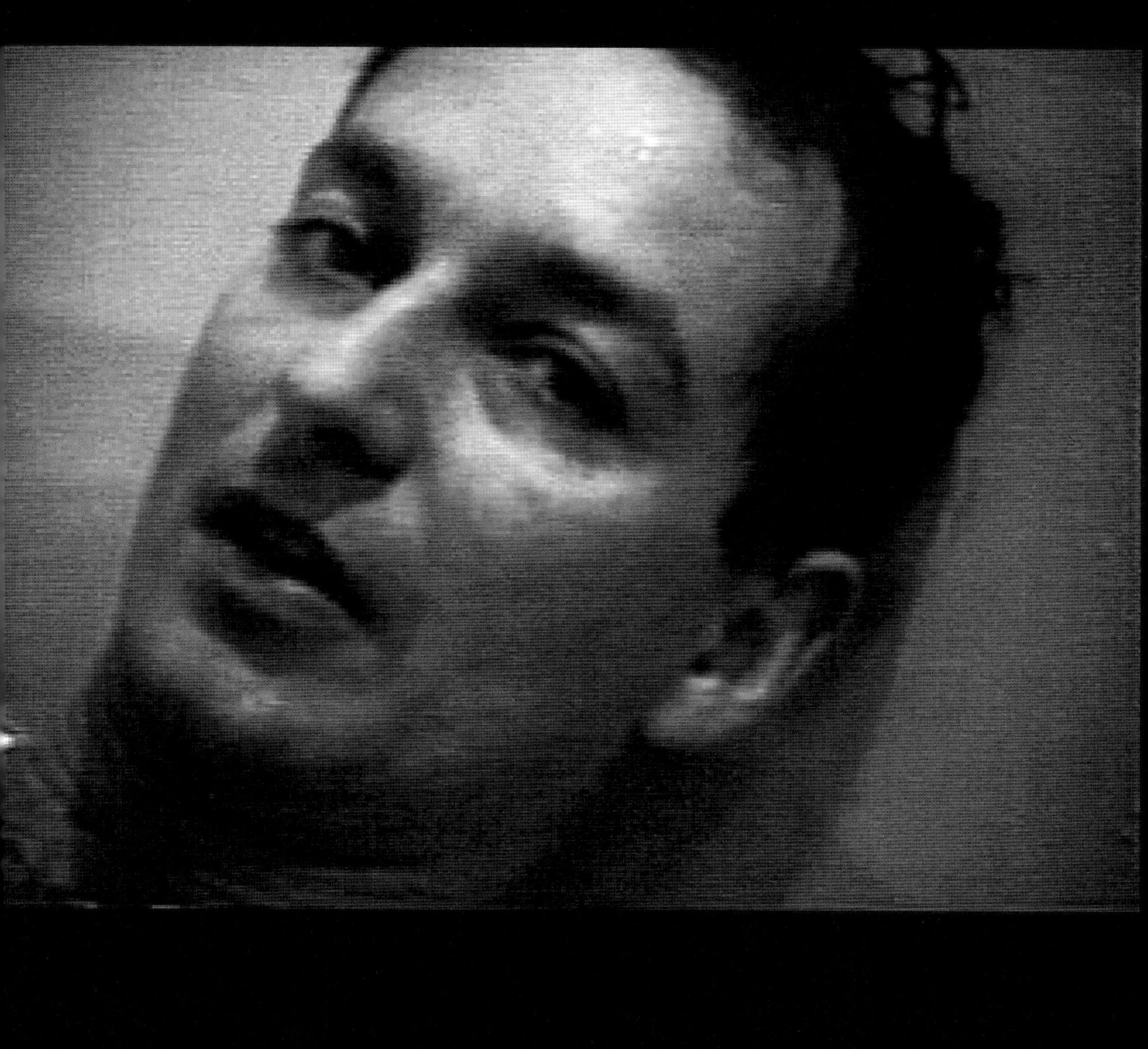

waiting for dave

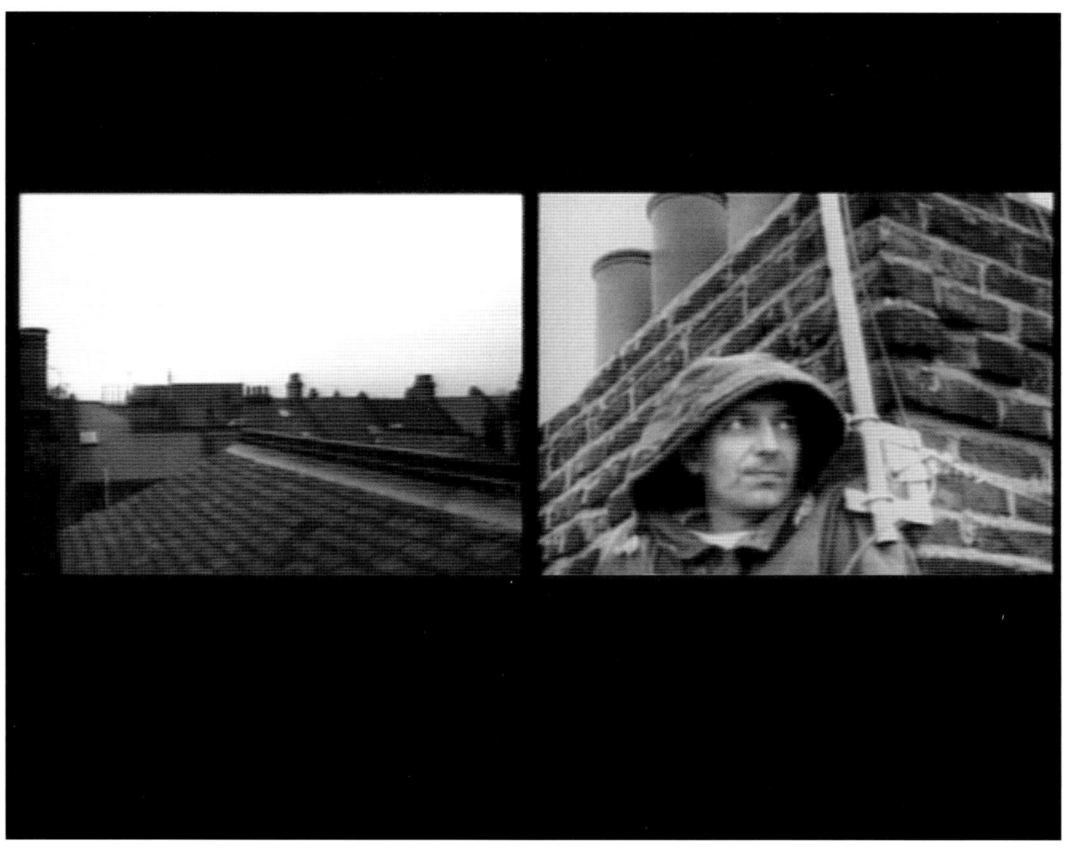

i was once involved in a shit show

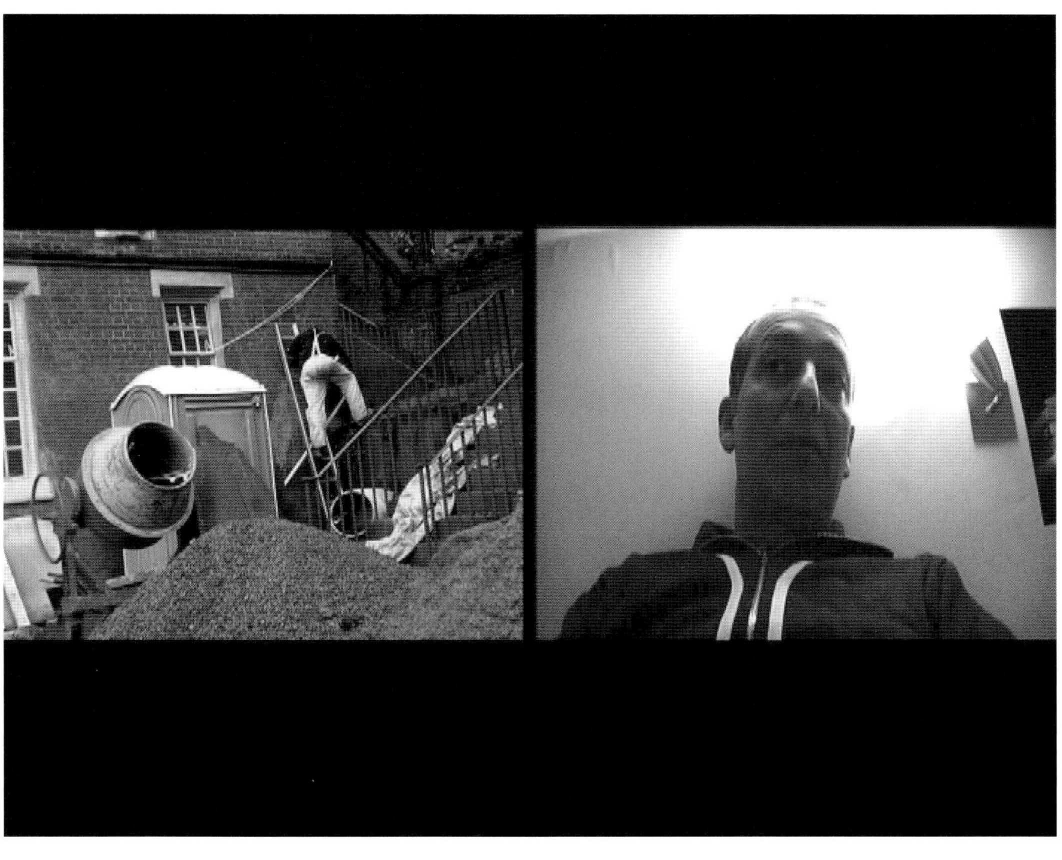

river sky

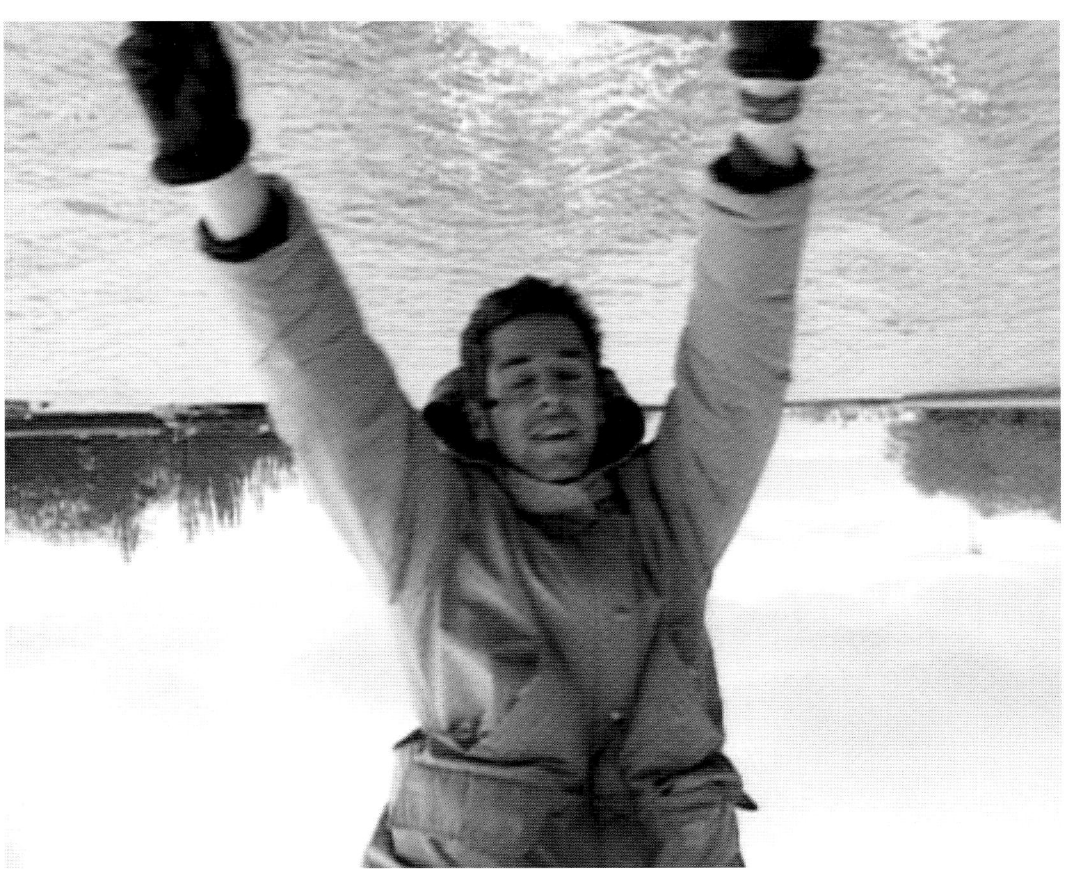

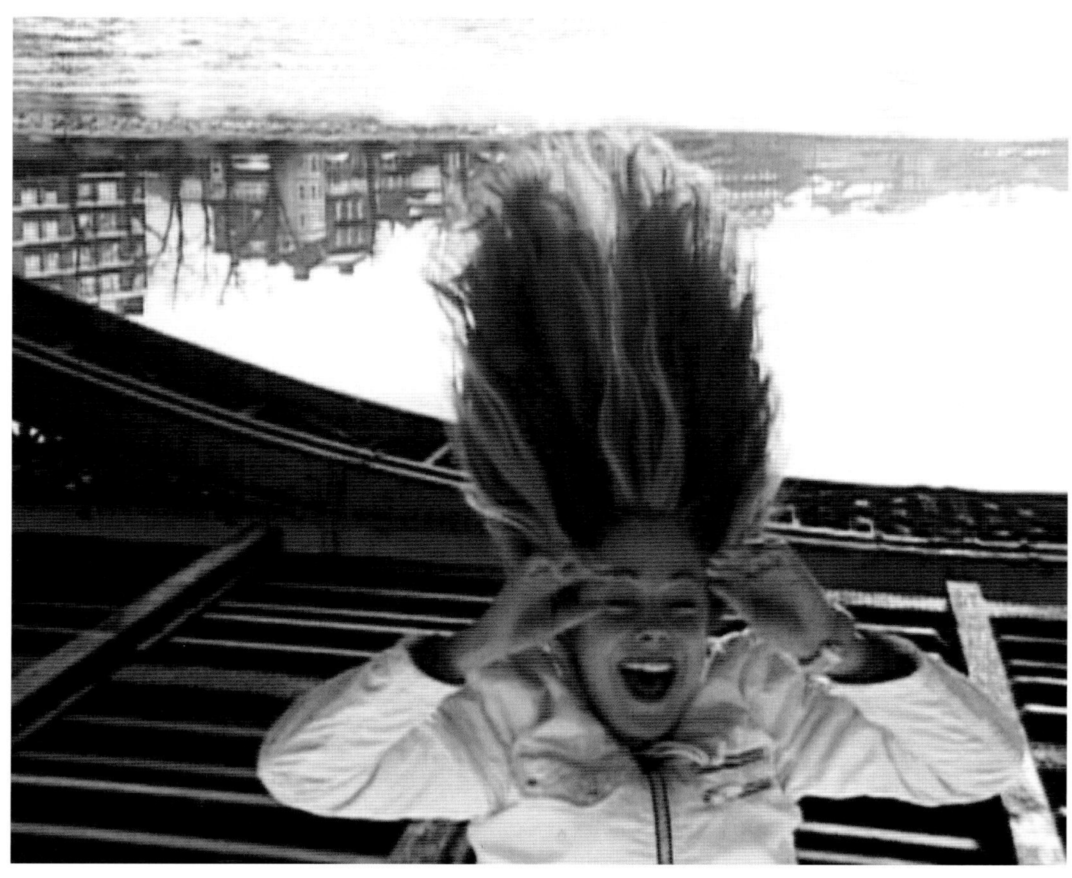

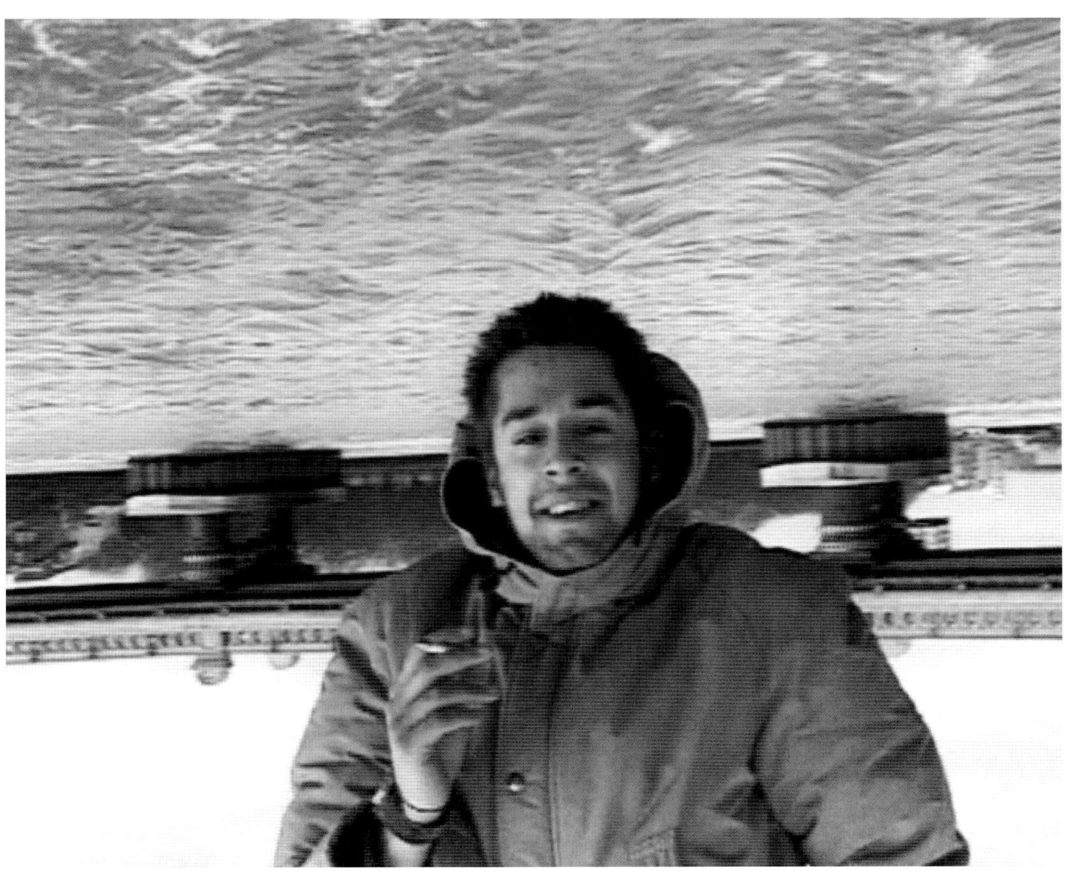

george barber: if you like, you can repeat the search with the omitted results included

paul morley

George Barber's films make me think about films. His films make me think about films that are between three and fifteen minutes long. About films that have no middle, beginning or end, not even in the wrong order. They don't really begin, and they don't as such end, and there's no absolute middle. His films make me think about how films capture life, and sometimes the life just dies, and other times the life seems to stay alive. His films show how things can happen before they've even happened.

Barber's films (or videos, or video-films) make me think of different moving surfaces culled from various sources being laid over one another to create stories about time, existence and motion that have nothing to do with the original material and its original context. He makes me think of the gaps in conversation, the shape of people's mouths, the sound their voices make when they're not actually saying anything, when they're stuttering, or shouting, or swallowing. The videos (or short films, or medium-length collections of images) make me think about confusion and also about bodies, and trees, and colour. About being lost, being angry, being bored, being trapped between today and all of my memories, between one moment and the next.

George's films (or long videos, or video films running at exactly the right length) make me think what it must be like to experience time in a completely different way: where the past, the present and the future all happened at the same time; where we might see and hear what happened, what is happening and what will happen all in one go. We might also be upside down. We might also be being filmed. We might also not have much to say about the experience. We might not remember that we are being filmed. We might not know that the way we are being filmed will eventually be used in ways we never anticipated.

They are films that say, we don't pass through time. Time passes through us.

They are films that say an awful lot about very little/ a very little about an awful lot.

Barber's films make me think about fact that what we think of as reality is always on the edge of collapsing. They make me think of ordinary moments and frozen moments and moments that mix into other moments and then repeat themselves and then just stop.

Barber's films make me think of the blog phenomenon on the web, where people write every day about things that interest them. Some of the things they write about are very interesting, and some are not interesting at all, which is actually quite fascinating. Sometimes they don't really have much to say about anything but feel they have to say something, and end up saying it quite beautifully.

There's no real point to what they write, other than the fact that they thought of doing it, and they thought that someone, somewhere, might be interested.

2/

I find myself being interviewed for television occasionally about art, and music, and entertainment, and what happened where, when and why. The interview I record will be chopped up into moments – hours of talking can turn into minutes can turn into simply pauses – and then scattered amongst many other people whose interviews have also been broken into bits and scattered about. Somehow out of all these broken bits of conversation built up into some rough narrative a kind of fragile sense emerges that just about clings to the possible idea of meaning.

I imagine if I ever got asked about the work of George Barber for one of these programmes – it could be the top ten scratch video makers of all time, or a short film entitled 'What About Copyright', or a study of artist film-makers whose subject is time, or a documentary about lonely men who find things to do in their spare time that might actually make them even lonelier – I might say:

Doubting, fearing, sensing impending doom, Barber lives in a fragmented world devoid of true understanding of the world around him, and his films accurately reflect this state of spiritual fragmentation and incompleteness. Indeed, it can be argued that Barber has yet to make a 'film', and that he is actually continuously in the act of making a film and that his resultant films serve to document this ongoing process. He is, if anything, restless, edgy, cowardly, perturbed, disturbed and uncertain, reflecting, in his own way, the words of the French philosopher Blaise Pascal, written over three centuries ago:

'When I consider the short duration of my life, swallowed up in the eternity before and after, the little space I fill, and even can see, engulfed in the infinite immensity of space of which I am ignorant, and which knows me not, I am frightened, and am astonished at being here rather than there, and why now rather than then.'

This would be shown in the programme as me simply saying:

He is actually continuously in the act of making a film.

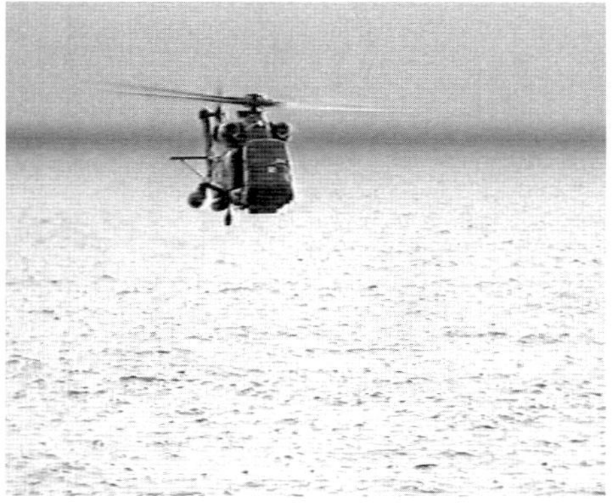

3/

One of George's films makes me think a lot about people who are trapped in their lives, trapped in unbelievable circumstances, and/or trapped inside the film *Airport '77*.

4/

I must say that this movie had a lot of potential to it.

Luckily for all of us, George Kennedy is at hand, as ever, to work out a solution to the crisis and thus bring the film to a not very gripping conclusion.

Not exactly plane sailing.

Plot:
The film starts with an array of rich film stars playing an array of rich stars boarding a luxury plane. Eventually the plane crashes into the water and sinks to the bottom. Will the crew and passengers survive?

The movie was very well done. The injury scenes with a lot of the passengers helping the injured were well acted.

747 impersonates a fish.

The plane is piloted by Jack Lemmon — looking very depressed, and who can blame him?

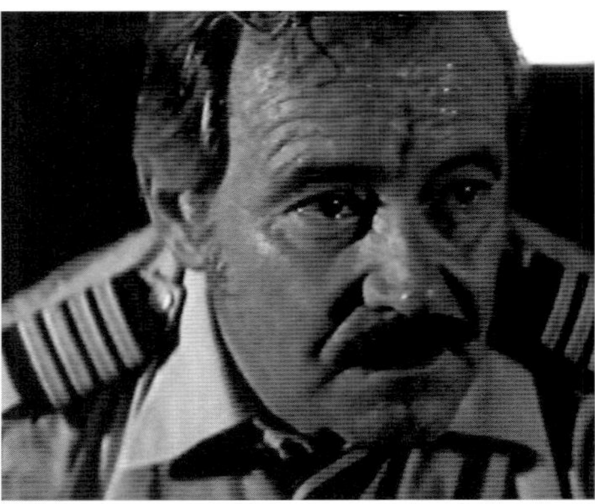

Lee Grant has the honour of the worst written role in the film as an unfaithful woman with Christopher Lee looking bored as her husband.

George Kennedy inexplicably shows up halfway through and starts ordering people around.

The take-off scene, as seen from outside, is the same as in *Airport '75*.

Characters:
Most of the cast are reduced to screaming hysterically, or being thrown about the plane.

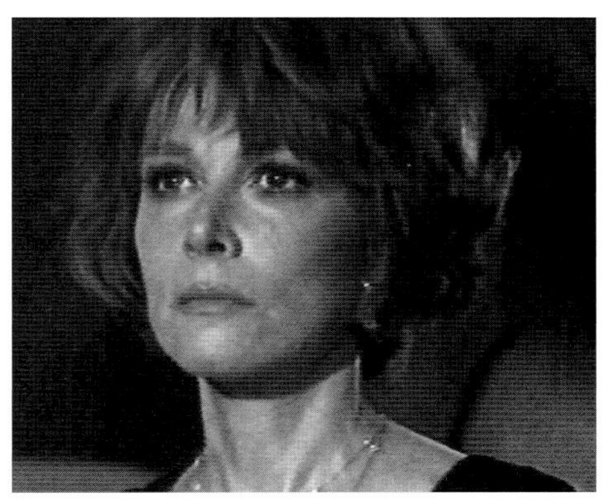

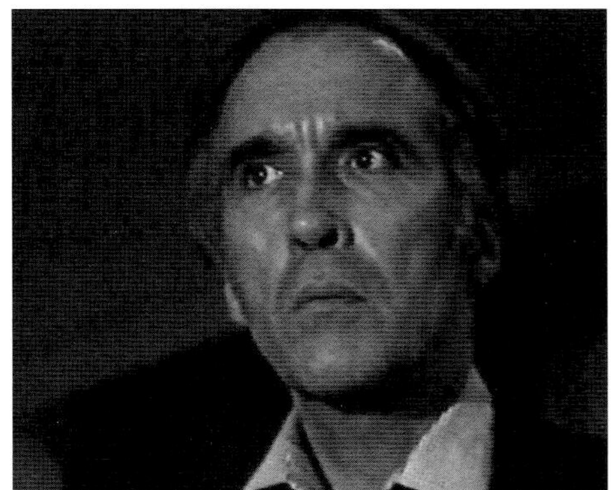

Some will live, others will die.

Unfortunately, nobody told director Jerry Jameson.

Joan Crawford was initially offered the part of 'Emily Livingston' in this all-star-cast disaster picture about a 747 loaded with VIPs that is hijacked and then crashes in the Bermuda Triangle. Said Joan: 'I wanted Joel McCrea to play opposite me, and anyway, they actually asked me to fly out there with only one week's notice! Why, that is hardly enough time for makeup tests or rehearsals... and when I asked about costume fittings, they said they wanted me to wear my own clothes!'

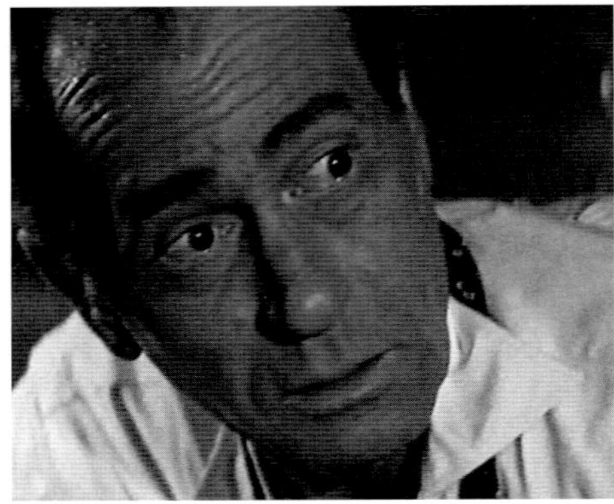

Joe Patroni (George Kennedy) began his career in aviation as the head of airport maintenance in the original *Airport*; his leadership of the snow removal crew ultimately saves the day for the unlucky plane.

In the melee, the plane goes out of control and dives into the ocean over the Bermuda Triangle.

Will the hijackers succeed in their dastardly plot?

A lot of injuries, a heck of a lot of water, and a rescue mission that is unbelievable, but achievable.

The scene where the plane goes down in the ocean is a pretty scary moment. After the plane submerges under water, the question becomes, will there be a rescue of the passengers in time, or will the plane fill up with water or run out of air before the rescue team gets to them?

The aircraft:
It is a private Boeing 747-100 owned by the Stevens Corporation, bearing the American Airlines basic colours, registry N23S. It is flying from Washington Dulles (IAD) to Palm Beach (PBI).

But it is mildly diverting, even if only for the appalling quality of the dialogue.

The quality of the video transfer on *Airport '77* is quite good. The colours are bright and strong, with only minor hints of a contrast problem. The Pan & Scan presentation is terrible however, making us all seasick from watching the horrible composition.

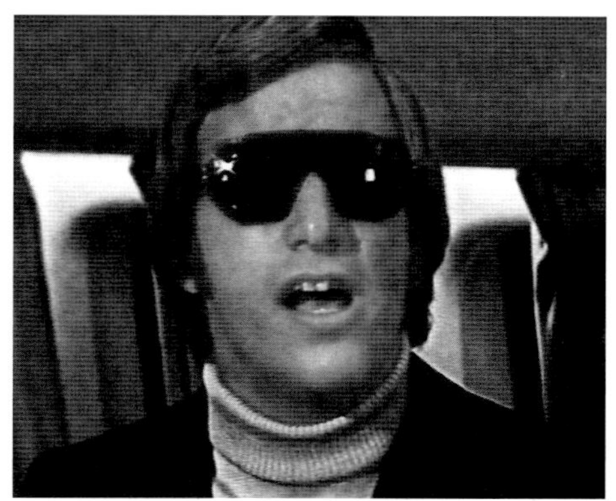

Jumbo jet goes Titanic.

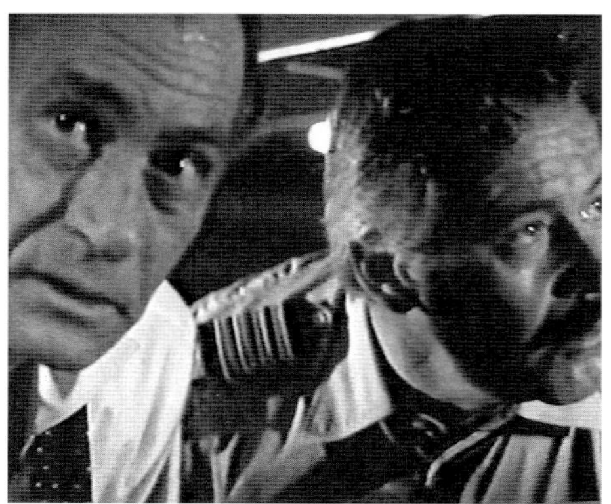

Lemmon appeared in dozens of high-profile films over 50 years, including comedies like *Some Like It Hot* (1959, with Marilyn Monroe and Tony Curtis) and dramas like *The Days of Wine* and *Roses* (1962), *Missing* (1982), *Glengarry Glen Ross* (1992) and even *Airport '77* (1977).

In *Airport '75*, Patroni was, inexplicably, a helicopter pilot who helped Charlton Heston rappel into the hole in the side of the plane.

A luxury 747 carrying valuable artwork is hijacked and lands in the ocean, submerged in shallow water.

11:37

So very tired. So much bean dip inside of me and so very tired... oh, look: Barbra Streisand. She looks lovely and heavy-set. Perhaps this is the Wayne Rogers tribute I've been reading about... Nope, just the Best Picture Award... Damn! *Airport '77* loses again. The Oscars are so overrated.

The film ultimately featured Jack Lemmon, James Stewart, Joseph Cotten (in the would-be McCrea role), Lee Grant, and Olivia de Havilland in the Livingston role.

While the passengers remain alive in the shallow water a daring rescue operation is planned to bring the plane up without breaking it in two.

How many deaths in the film? 4 to 8.

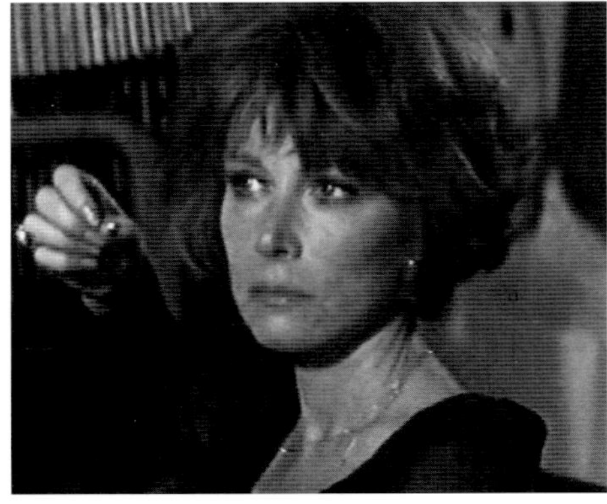

1974: Lee excellent as assassin Scaramanga in James Bond film *The Man With the Golden Gun*.

Will the crew and passengers make it out before the plane floods with water?

It's scary because it can easily happen to you.

Any profanity? Occasional swearing.

Upon close inspection, it appears that other than the actual title art, there is no red colour to the picture at all, which would account for the overly blue appearance.

On video, George Kennedy only appears three times throughout the movie, but on the TV version, extra footage is added and he is in the beginning of the movie as well.

Even though most people consider the original *Airport* picture to be the best, I think *Airport '77*, the third movie in the series, is far and away the best. This is a very entertaining movie about an airplane crashing into the ocean.

For the same film, legendary costume designer Edith Head won the Best Costume Design Award, her first of eight career Oscars. She would win Best Costume Design honours seven more times, in 1950 (twice), in 1951, in 1953, in 1954, in 1960, and in 1973. [She would be nominated each year (and sometimes twice) from 1948 to 1966 for Costume Design — an unprecedented accomplishment! By her final film *Airport '77*, she had a total of 35 nominations in the category.]

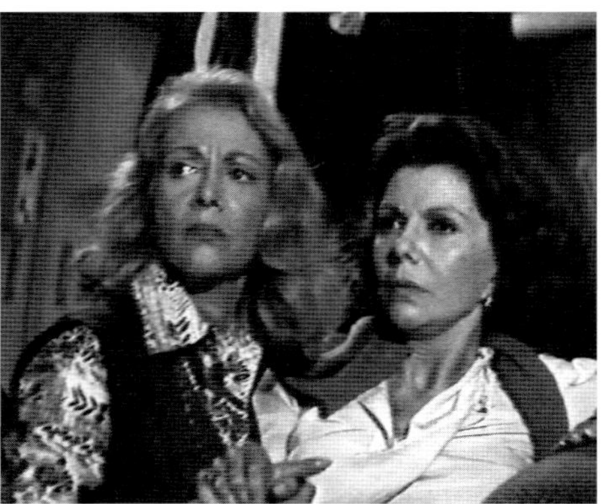

But when hijackers take over the plane and knock everyone out with sleeping gas, the plane crashes in the sea and
survives but a small hole at the front is flooding the plane
and two daring rescues must be put into action because
everyone is trapped 200 feet underwater.

**In *Airport '77*, I'm not sure what Joe Patroni was, but he
hung out with the Navy guys in the radar room and wore
a headset.**

He then says 'Jesus Christ!', in a state of shock and possibly
fear too. The plane's nose is then lowered in order to gain
speed, I assume to stop the stalling, but it crashes into the
ocean, causing it to sink.

Waterlogged stars escape plane.

Will ageing lovers Joseph Cotten and Olivia De Havilland
reunite for one last attempt to rake over the embers of their
passion?

**A prototype commercial 747, en route for a museum
opening in Palm Beach, is hijacked and crashes into the
Bermuda Triangle. The pilot (Jack Lemmon) and Chief
Executive (Brenda Vacarro) must keep the passengers
safe and sane while awaiting rescue. Pilot Don Gallagher
(Lemmon) enlists the aid of stalwart entrepreneur
(Christopher Lee) to help him launch a lifeboat to the
surface of the water.**

Lee and Lee argue.

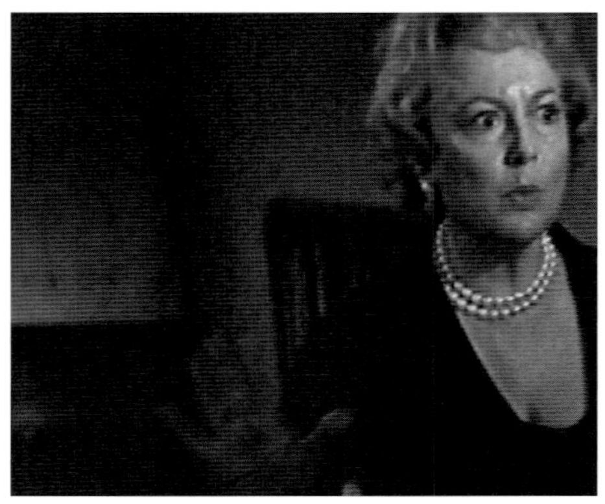

Effects:
For 1977, the effects are quite impressive. The beginning is actually quite exciting if not scary, when the plane plunges into the sea. From then on the film tries hard to build suspense and develop the characters. There is nothing special here, and only towards the end is the excitement and tension restored once more.

Advantages: enjoyable, good effects.
Disadvantages: poor acting, lots of screaming.

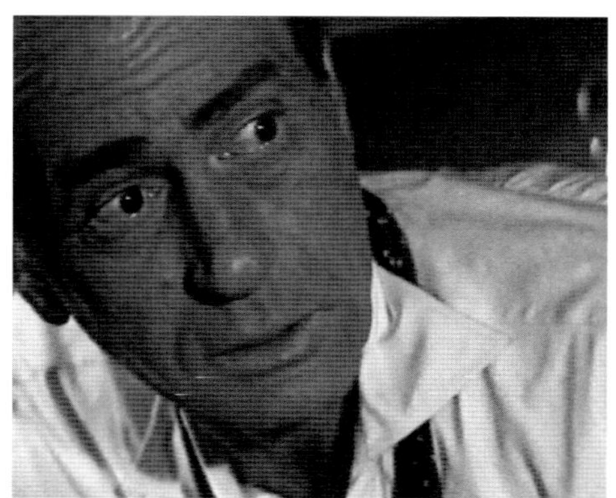

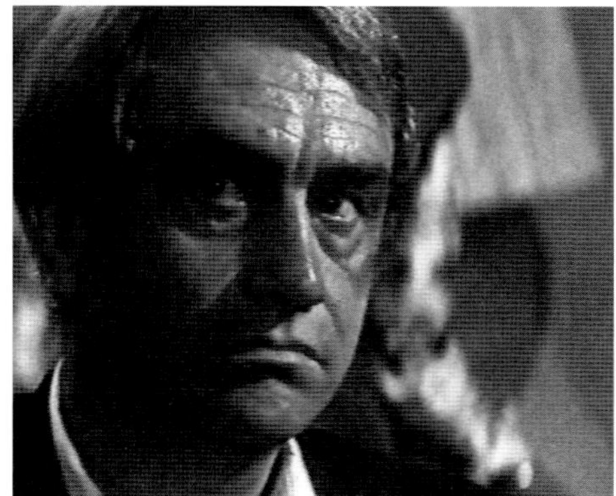

Jimmy Stewart plays Stevens, a rich businessman whose daughter and granddaughter are on the flight. He doesn't do much except look really, really worried.

1975: Lee reprised the Rochefort role for Lester's *The Four Musketeers*.

George Kennedy — the only actor to appear in all four of the series.

Jameson is a close #2 behind Irwin Allen in the sheer amount of disaster crud he's dumped on the public. He also directed *Airport '77*, *Raise the Titanic!*, and a whole slew of TV disaster movies with titles like *Terror on the 40th Floor* and *The Deadly Tower* and *The Elevator*.

1977: Lee appeared in *Airport '77* as famous oceanographer Martin Wallace, henpecked by his boozy wife Lee Grant.

A further follow-up, *Airport '77* (1977), pushed the suspension of disbelief to ever more bizarre levels, in this case a 747 which crashes in the Atlantic and sinks, trapping everyone on board under water.

The rescue capabilities of the Navy in this movie were real by the way.

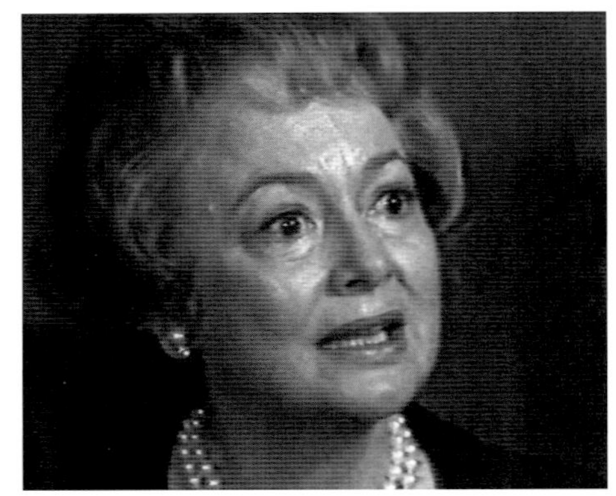

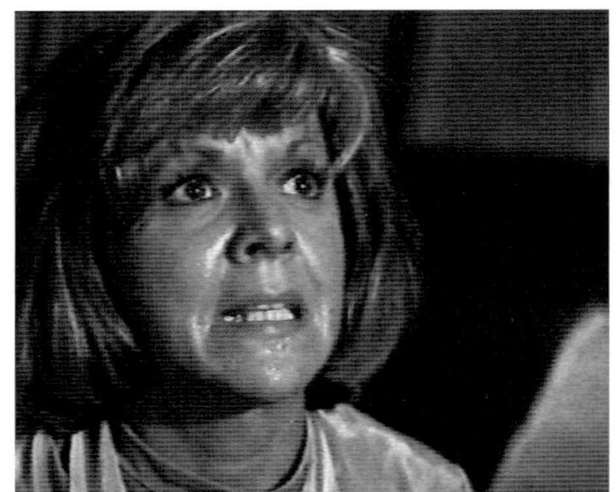

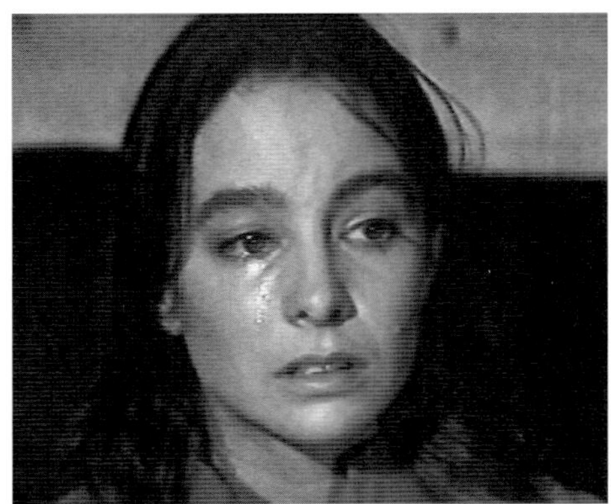

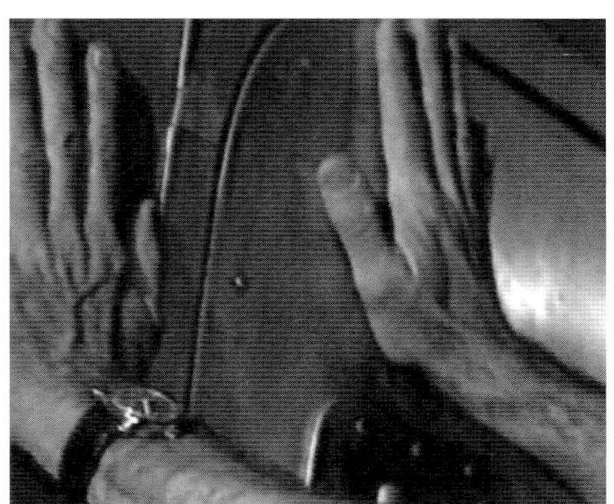

In *Airport '79: The Concorde*, Joe Patroni has changed careers again. Now he's a pilot. Everyone keeps calling him fat, which is a drag.

5/

George Barber's films make me think that you can have two, or three, or four images at the same time, in much the same way you can have two, or three, or four ideas at the same time. Sometimes an image can repeat itself in the way that an idea repeats itself. Sometimes the image doesn't really go anywhere in the way that an idea might go nowhere. His films make me think of something that someone once said, or something I think someone should have said, or something I once said when interviewed sometime in the future about the films of George Barber, films which record things that never quite happened, or if they did, were not filmed. His films say that you must save what you can of life, save what fragments of life you can amidst the present nonsensical conditions of everyday existence. His films are small, random, odd parts of life, of thoughts about life, of nothing much in particular, of all that we have, which is our lingering sense of each other, saved in the form of film, saved in the way that images can frame memory, and movement, and ultimately stillness.

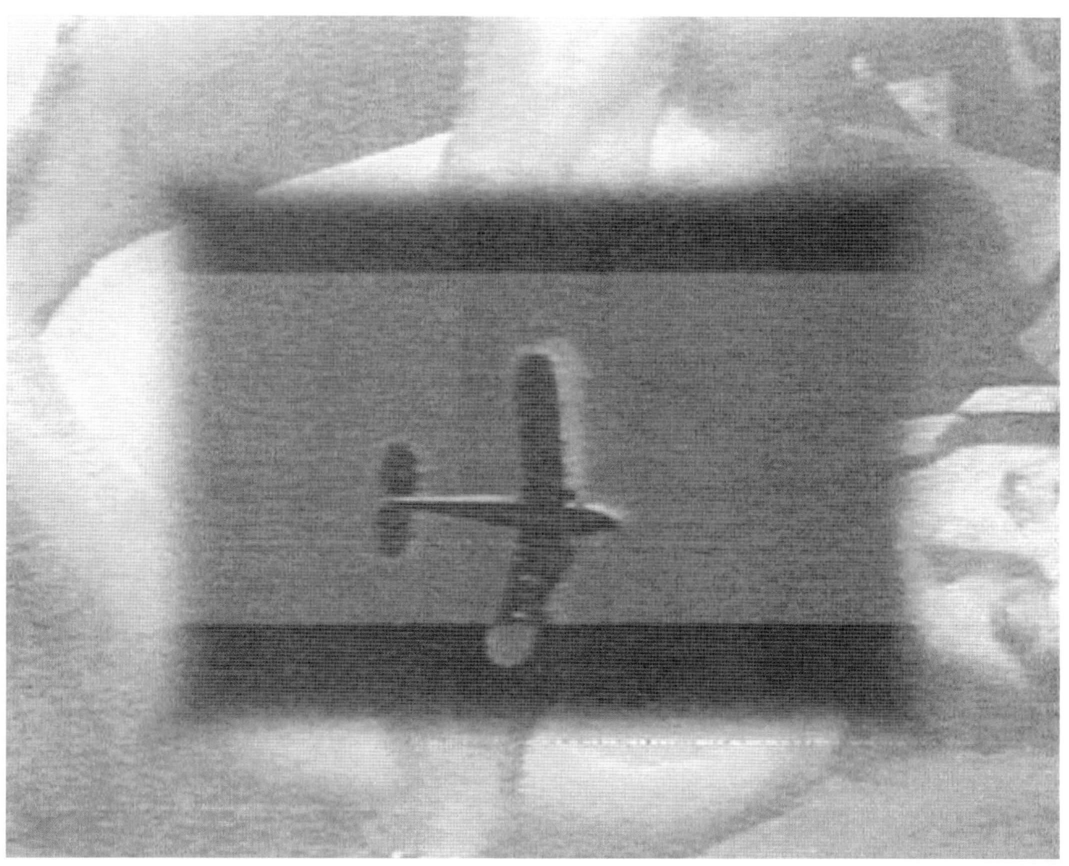

6/

One of George's films made me think that it's terribly hard knowing quite how to act in front of other people, and indeed how hard it is knowing how to act in front of actors. It also made me think that when you watch Alan Rickman acting you are never quite sure if he is taking himself too seriously, or not seriously enough.

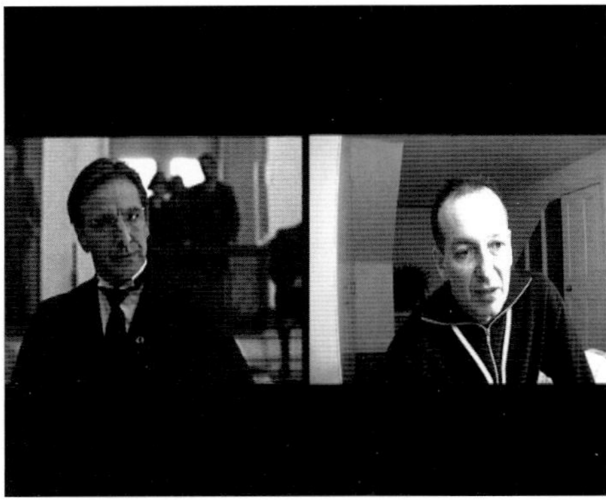

7/

For youngsters, Rickman is Harry Potter's Professor Snape, the teacher that's never as evil as he appears. But he doesn't want to talk about it.

What is the other main ingredient of champ with potatoes?
Alan Rickman.

Next I visited the whole-foods store in my Notting Hill neighbourhood. Apparently, this is the place to be on a Saturday afternoon. Yuppie mums-to-be sauntered in and out with their golden Labradors. I (literally) bumped into British actor Alan Rickman sifting through organic spices. But the prices!

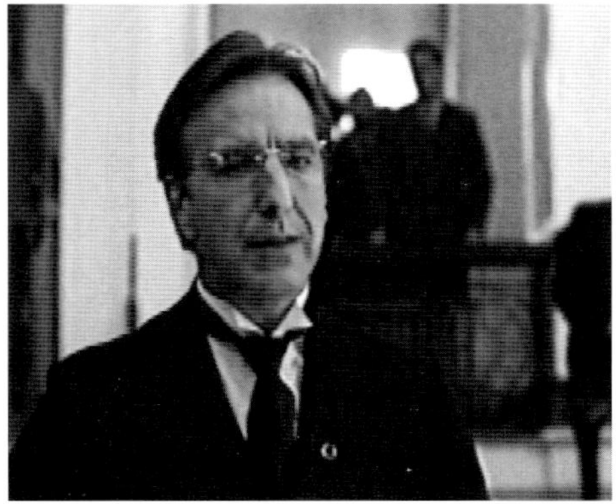

From an early age, creativity and intelligence shone in the young Alan Rickman. As a child, he scribbled and doodled and had elegant calligraphy and talent in creating watercolour paintings.

'I spend my life acting,' explained Alan Rickman.

'And ten pounds of potatoes among other things is not so good for my back,' remarked Alan Rickman.

What can you tell us about the new Harry Potters?
I don't talk about Harry Potter.

Does anybody besides Emily and me find Alan Rickman
totally hot?
Also, Wendy tried to convince me that oysters were the
potatoes of the sea…

But you're in the third one?
Yes.
Have they started on the fourth one?
They have. I haven't.
Will you be in it?
Eventually…

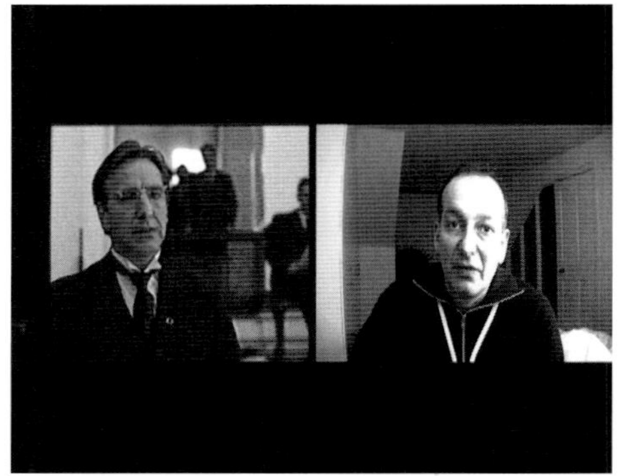

Alan Rickman lost a stone (14lb/6kg) in that time, and
if he can do it, on a diet without bread, cereal, milk,
alcohol, potatoes and…

It's only with Penelope (Keith), Alan (Rickman), and Simon
(Callow) that the fun really started — Rickman moans
about Helen Mirren stealing his mashed potatoes…

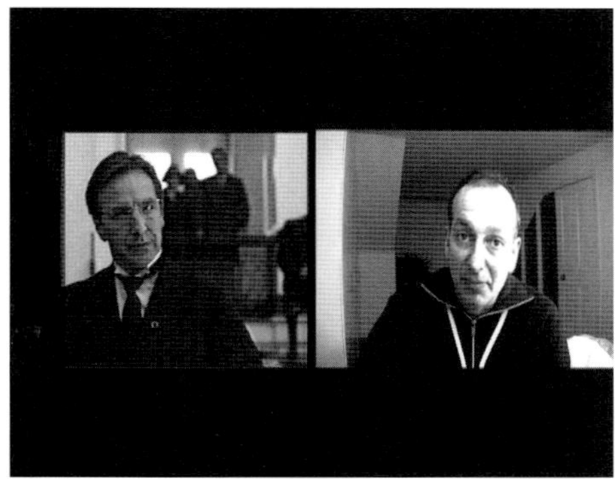

I wasn't expecting any more than a chance to stare at Alan Rickman and when you haven't got any slaves, you have to dig your own potatoes...

Favourite Actors and Actresses: Johnny Depp, Winona Ryder, Alan Rickman, Uma Thurman.
Favourite Food: Potatoes!

The actors Terry is thinking of are Jeffrey Jones and Alan Rickman and potatoes that look like President Eisenhower.

'The thinking woman's sex symbol' Alan Rickman has a delicious dinner of steak tips & potatoes.

And the pride of Great Britain, Tim Henman, lost again to Alan Rickman, who is tempted by his secretary.

I met George Barber at a party once. The party was at the home of a television producer. I remember that Jeremy Vine, the ex-presenter of *Newsnight* now a disc jockey on Radio 2, in fact the replacement for Jimmy Young, was there, but I didn't talk to him. I didn't really talk to anyone as such, always finding it difficult to know how to act in front of people at parties, people who are often strangers but who you must greet and treat as if they are old friends.

I find this kind of small talk difficult, as I assume that a) no one is interested in me, and b) I am possibly not interested in the people at the parties. Also, I feel I have used up my small talk, that I am drained of considering just how to lubricate a conversation with a total stranger so that the brief swapping of information about our lives doesn't plummet like a stone into the abyss of existence and make the parting that will eventually happen, and quite soon too, extremely difficult to achieve in a way that isn't profoundly uncomfortable. I tend to end up at parties standing in the corners, up against walls, looking as if I am suffering, chronically, possibly from some sort of autism, a party autism. Perhaps this affliction has some kind of name — partism. I have noticed that when I was younger and drank a lot more this partism wasn't so obvious, and that my partism has increased the older I have got, because the older I have got the less I have drunk. Somehow, the shyness I have, which obviously projects itself in party circumstances as a kind of shady adolescent arrogance, hasn't dispelled now that I am embedded in grumbling middle age.

I met George at the party, but actually I had met him before, about twenty years before. I don't remember any-thing about that meeting, and didn't recognise him when he started talking to me, until the moment he introduced himself, when I remembered remembering that we had met, at some point, about something. I wish the original meeting had been filmed, actually saved, so that my memory of it could be refreshed every so often, and I could marvel at the change in my appearance over the years. The American actor Bill Murray calls this ageing process 'being poisoned' —

he says it is the only explanation for how your body and your hair and the spark in your eyes is so affected. You have changed so much in shape and manner there can be no other explanation. You have been poisoned. Poisoned, I suppose, by time. Time, therefore, is a poisonous thing. It poisons us, silently, quite rapidly, without us really noticing. At the time.

George didn't seem to be made uncomfortable by my partism. Perhaps he suffered, or enjoyed, his own form of partism, and so we connected, like two addicts, happy to grumble in the shadows and finding disturbed, disturbing areas of compatibility. He saved me at that party from what would have seemed like a lifetime of standing at the edge of everything, looking in, wondering how to negotiate my way into the centre of a conversation that actually had some kind of fluency.

Perhaps the way I open small talk can be faulted. After I am introduced to someone I sometimes end up saying:

'The more the Universe seems comprehensible, the more it also seems pointless.'

Silence will ensue. A parting of the ways. The aroma of embarrassment spreading throughout the room on its way to the rest of the Universe, which is pointless and smells of embarrassment.

George didn't appear too bothered with my gothic small talk. His own small talk trembled on the edge of the gloomy too.

Very soon we were chatting away as if we had known each other for years, which in a way, I suppose we had. Perhaps the last time we had met, we got on very well, and ended up as friends, but I don't remember, because the meeting hadn't been filmed. We talked about, I think, tennis, and futility, and wine, and roses — we ended up in the garden, staring up at the night sky as if the relief we felt at finding a party buddy somehow made life seem richer, sweeter, lovelier.

We ended up hugging each other as we said goodbye. We swapped numbers and details and carried on talking about tennis, and skin problems, and the English puritans who settled Massachusetts in the early 1600s.

I didn't see George again until we both found ourselves on the banks of the River Thames watching the illusionist David Blaine climb out of a plastic box where he had been locked away for a few weeks. It was 2002, or 3, but surely not 4. Blaine climbed unsteadily out of the box as if he had just been rescued from a Jumbo Jet that had crashed into the ocean and sunk. He looked as if time had poisoned him very severely — years of poison, as opposed to a few weeks of poison. For the illusionist, a few weeks had seemed like a few years, which is a hell of an illusion.

He had the stunned, fearful look of a man who had been trapped under water for close to eternity sharing a small space with a hostile Christopher Lee and a miserable Jack Lemmon with the threat of drowning, and the bulk of George Kennedy, never far away. He'd played endless tennis with James Stewart and his world turned upside down and he didn't want to say anything to anyone — he just wanted to shout, and shout, and shout. He'd called Joan Crawford a million times but always got her answer machine. His eyes stared out into nowhere as if inside the box he had fully realised that not only is the Universe pointless, but all of human history as well. All the time he was inside the box being engulfed by the infinite immensity of space, mocked by ghosts, abused by passers by, poisoned by time, he had been filmed.

George and I didn't say much to each other. There wasn't much to say, but then, it's not clear there ever is, and watching the feeble David Blaine, who had come close to starving himself to death for the sake of entertainment in a plastic box above the River Thames, obviously made us sink deep into our own private thoughts, which are mercilessly shaped by our own sense of space, and time, and memory. Perhaps George was preoccupied by what he could do with all that footage of the trapped illusionist. Perhaps he was worried that Alan Rickman was following him, taking notes.

We said goodbye but we didn't hug.
I haven't seen George since then.

lists

George Barber
Born 1958, Georgetown, Guyana
Studied at St. Martin's School of Fine Art, London and
the Slade School of Fine Art, London
Lives and works in London

SOLO SHOWS
2004   'New Work', Gallery West, London
        Shouting Match, Open Eye Gallery, Liverpool
        Upside Down Minutiae and *Yes Frank, No Smoke,* Galerie Contemporain
        Centre Regional d'Art, Sete, France

GROUP SHOWS AND FESTIVALS
2005   *Shouting Match*, Rotterdam Film Festival
2004   *Shouting Match*, Winterthur Short Film Festival, Switzerland
        Shouting Match, World Wide Video Festival, Holland
        Walking Off Court, Melbourne International Film Festival
        'Scratch Vol. 2', Prenelle Gallery, London (part of part of the Island
        Film Festival)
        Tilt, Bloomberg Space, London (part of 'The Mind Is a Horse')
        Walking Off Court, European Media Art Festival, Osnabruck, Germany
        'Untitled', S1 Artspace, Sheffield
        River Sky, BCA Gallery, Bedford and Millais Gallery, Southampton
        (part of 'Unlimited Edition')
        Tilt, Tate Britain, London (part of 'A Century Of Artist's Film in Britain')
2003   *Walking Off Court*, Viper Festival, Switzerland, Media Art Festival
        Friesland, Holland, Split Film & Video Festival, Croatia and New York
        Video Festival
2002   *Walking Off Court* and *I Was Once Involved In A Shit Show*,
        World Wide Video Festival Holland
        LUX Open Show, Royal College Of Art
        Gate, Dartmoor
        'The Video Show', Anthony Wilkinson Gallery, London
2001   Toronto International Video Art Biennial
        'Video a Mi Gusto', Instituto de la Juventud, Madrid
        Upside Down Minutiae, European Media Art Festival, Osnabruck,
        Germany
        River Sky, ICA and National Film Theatre, London (part of
        'Unlimited Edition')
        River Sky, Viper Festival, Switzerland
        'Slipstream' (www.slipstream.uk.net), ICA, London
2000   'Discrepancy', Video Positive, Citadel St. Helens

1999   *Withdrawal*, Museum of Contemporary Art, Barcelona (part of 'Home
        Sweet Home')
        Impakt Festival, Utrecht, Netherlands
        Videofest, Berlin
1998   *Withdrawal*, New York Film & Video Festival, Video Positive, Liverpool,
        Viper Festival, Switzerland
        Effervescence, ICA, London (part of 'Fuzzy Logic')
1997   *Withdrawal*, ICA, London
        'Ripe', Bluecoat Gallery, Liverpool
        'Ansaphone', Whitechapel Open, London
        Arizona, World Wide Video Festival, W.R.O, Poland, Berlin, The Kitchen,
        New York, Dallas Video Festival, Centre for Arts Hobart, San Francisco
        International Film Festival, and London Film Festival
1996   Retrospective, ICA, London (part of the Pandemonium Festival)
        Passing Ship, Vigo Festival, Australian Film & Video Festival, World Wide
        Video Festival, Locarno Video Festival and Pompidou Centre Paris

BIBLIOGRAPHY
'Hanging Out With Artistry', Victor Lewis-Smith, *Evening Standard*,
        14th December UK, 2001
'Island that daren't face the music', Miles Kingston, *The Independent on Sunday*,
        24th March, UK, 1991
'This Week – First Person', Quentin Curtis, *The Independent on Sunday*,
        24th March, UK, 1991
'Cyberspace Video High Volume One', Jim McClellan, *The Observer*, UK, 1998
'Cyberspace Video High Volume One', Steve Beard, *ID Magazine*, UK, 1998
'George Barber' *A Directory of British Film & Video Artists*, David Curtis (ed.),
        The Arts Council of England, University of Luton Press, 1996
'George Barber Retrospective', Suzanne Moore, *Pandaemonium* (catalogue),
        London Electronic Arts, UK, 1996
'The Venetian Ghost', Steven Bode, *Independent Media*, Issue 77, 1988
'Cooking for Terrorists', Julian Petley, *New Statesman*, June, UK, 1988
'Il Fenomeno Scratch', Maria Rosa Sossai, *Videovibe*, Castelvecchi Arte, Italy, 1988
'Yes Frank, No Smoke', Michael O'Pray, *The Elusive Sign*, Arts Council of
        England/British Council, 1988
'Scratching Deeper', Michael O'Pray, *Art Monthly*, 1986

AWARDS
Grand Prix, Split Film & Video Festival, Croatia, 2004
Gold Award, ARS ELECTRONICA, Austria 1998
Gold Award, Chicago Film Festival, 1990

TV BROADCASTS

2001   *Upside Down Minutiae*, Slotart/Channel 4
1998   *The Weather*, Channel 4
1997   *Electric Passions*, Channel 4
1994   *The Happening History Of Video Art* (Director), The Late Show/BBC 2

BBC RADIO BROADCASTS

1999   *Collapse*, BBC World Service (experimental soundwork/drama)
1998   *Collapse*, BBC Radio 3 (experimental drama)
1998   *Accidents Will Happen*, BBC Radio 4 (documentary series)
1997   *The Locker Room*, BBC Radio 4

SELECTED VIDEOGRAPHY

Refusing Potatoes, 6 min, 2004
Shouting Match, 11 min, 2004
Walking Off Court, 11 min, 2003
What's That Sound?, 3 min, 2003
I Was Once Involved In A Shit Show, 7 min, 2003
River Sky, 4 min, 2002
Upside Down Minutiae, 6 min, 2000
Discrepancy, 15 min, 2000
Withdrawal, 5 min, 1997
The Weather, 5 min, 1997
Ansaphone, 7 min, 1996
1001 Colours Andy Never Thought Of, 4 min, 1996
Simultaneous City (Liverpool), 6 min, 1996
Passing Ship, 6 min, 1996
Arizona, 5 min, 1995
Curtain Trip, 5 min, 1994
Waiting for Dave, 6 min, 1994
Jazzland, 4 min, 1992
Taxi Driver II, 7 min, 1987
Yes Frank, No Smoke, 6 min, 1985
Absence of Satan, 4 min, 1985
Branson, 2 min, 1984
Scratch Free State, 4 min, 1983
Tilt, 4 min, 1983
Divorce, 7 min, 1982